Traditional Ties

CULTURAL AWARENESS AND LISTENING SKILLS

Traditional Ties

CULTURAL AWARENESS AND LISTENING SKILLS

Silvia Bégin
Philippa Bianco
Ardiss Mackie

A RADIO PLAY

Longman

Traditional Ties: Cultural Awareness and Listening Skills

Longman, 95 Church Street, White Plains, N.Y. 10601

Associated companies:
Longman Group Ltd., London
Longman Cheshire Pty., Melbourne
Longman Paul Pty., Auckland
Copp Clark Pitman, Toronto

Distributed in the United Kingdom by Longman Group
Ltd., Longman House, Burnt Mill, Harlow, Essex CM20
2JE, England and by associated companies, branches,
and representatives throughout the world.

Executive editor: Joanne Dresner
Development editor: Karen Davy, Penny Laporte
Production editor: Lisa Hutchins
Text design adaptation: Publication Services, Inc.
Cover design: Joseph DePinho.
Text art: Publication Services, Inc. and Leslie Dunlap
Production supervisor: Anne Armeny

Library of Congress Cataloging in Publication Data
Bégin, Silvia.
    Traditional ties: cultural awareness and listening skills: a radio
play / Silvia Bégin, Philippa Bianco, Ardiss Mackie.
        p.   cm.
    ISBN 0-8013-0816-X
    1. English language—Textbooks for foreign speakers.   2. Life
skills—Problems, exercises, etc.   3. Radio plays, American.
4. Readers—Life skills.   5. Listening.   I. Bianco, Philippa.
II. Mackie, Ardiss.   III. Title.
PE1128.B4187   1992
428.3'4—dc20   91-41026
                                                       CIP

1 2 3 4 5 6 7 8 9 10-AL-9695949392

We would like to dedicate this book to Ardiss's mother, Elizabeth, to Philippa's parents, Elisabeth and Roy, and to Silvia's husband, Germain, and sister, Liliana.

Contents

Introduction

~~~~~~

Designed for low-intermediate students of English as a second language, *Traditional Ties* is a radio drama that incorporates cultural awareness and an exciting, romantic storyline. *Traditional Ties* is suitable for the classroom as well as for self-study. Although the focus of the text is listening, the activities integrate cultural awareness, other language skills, and life skills.

TEACHING TRADITIONAL TIES ~~~~~~~~~~~~~~~~~

The episode sequence must be respected in order to present the storyline. Each of the ten episodes is divided into parts. A part consists of listening activities (identified by a cassette symbol) with related reading, writing, and speaking activities. Each part presents a new piece of the story to advance the plot.

Before listening to the episode for the first time, students are asked to *Think Back* and summarize the key events of the preceding episode.

The *Take a Guess* activities ask students to predict events by looking at visuals, the title, or other clues.

In preparation for each new activity, students should first read the entire exercise before listening to the tape. New vocabulary can be presented before the listening; or the students can be asked to infer meaning through context during listening.

There are three types of listening exercises for each part of an episode. *Have You Got It?* facilitates general comprehension of the story. *Check It Out* and *Double-Check It* focus on more detail the second and third time the part is played.

The follow-up activities are not essential to following the storyline. *Traditional Ties* can be used as a text uniquely for listening comprehension and enjoyment. It can also be used by students to enrich their understanding of North American culture and help develop life skills essential for anyone living in that culture. This is the aim of the follow-up activities in each part.

In *Did You Get That?* exercises, students develop their vocabulary by listening again to functional language from the episode.

Work It Out includes problem-solving activities to expand language and life skills used in the story.

By focusing on the relationships between the characters in the storyline, *Between the Lines* gives students an opportunity to develop skills for making inferences.

The activities in *What Do You Think?* are designed to help students draw conclusions and make judgments about events and characters in the story.

What About You? asks students to consider their reactions to and feelings about the storyline and to talk about how they might behave in a similar situation.

In Other Words helps students infer the meaning of vocabulary and everyday expressions from context.

Act It Out offers students a chance to role play events related to the episode.

Body Language focuses on the cultural differences in body language by asking students to make comparisons among the cultures they come from.

The *Let's Talk About*... activities are related to the cultural component presented in each part of the episode. This cultural exercise is offered with a word of caution. It is difficult to represent the entire English-speaking North American context in a few lines. Expectations vary among social classes, locales, generations, and gender. We have selected but one aspect and hope the teacher will expand on other aspects as needed.

ACKNOWLEDGMENTS

We would like to thank Lorne Kirkwold for his contribution to the storyline
of the book. We are also grateful to the editorial staff at Longman for their
helpful comments and suggestions.

Breaking the Ice

PART ONE

◆ TAKE A GUESS

Look at the picture. Then discuss these questions with your classmates.

1. Who are the people?
2. Where are they?
3. What are they doing?
4. What are marriages of convenience?

📼 HAVE YOU GOT IT?

Listen to the conversation. What are Sushila and her parents talking about? Check (✔) the topics.

a. ☐ a newspaper article

b. ☐ marriages of convenience

c. ☐ buying a house

d. ☐ food

📼 CHECK IT OUT

Listen again. Are these sentences correct? Check (✔) *Yes* or *No*. If *No*, correct the sentence. The first one is done for you.

	Yes	No

1. Marriages of convenience are ~~down~~ *up*.   ☐   ✔
2. Sushila thinks marriages of convenience are bad.   ☐   ☐
3. Sushila is going to the hockey game alone.   ☐   ☐
4. Sushila must be home by 11 o'clock.   ☐   ☐

📼 DOUBLE-CHECK IT

Listen again. What do Sushila and her parents say about marriages of convenience? Check (✔) your answers. The first one is done for you.

Marriages of convenience are for people who:

a. ✔ want to stay in another country.

b. ☐ are in love.

c. ☐ are in trouble in their country.

d. ☐ have daughters.

◆ WHAT ABOUT YOU?

People get married for many different reasons. In your opinion, why do people get married? Look at the list of reasons below. Discuss this list with a partner. Write *1* next to the best reason, *2* next to the next best reason, and so on. Add any other reasons.

People get married because:

_____ they are in love.

_____ their husband or wife has a lot of money.

_____ their families want them to marry.

_____ they want a passport for another country.

_____ they are going to have a baby.

_____ they have traditions such as arranged marriages.

_____ they want to have children later on.

_____ they will have a higher position in society.

_____ other _____

◆ BETWEEN THE LINES

Read the questions. Circle your answers. Then discuss your answers with your classmates.

1. How old is Sushila?

    a. in her early teens

    b. in her twenties

    c. over thirty

2. How do Sushila's parents treat her?

    a. like a child

    b. like an adult

    c. like a friend

3. How does she feel about being treated like this?

    a. excited

    b. unhappy

    c. scared

◆ LET'S TALK ABOUT . . . PARENTS AND CHILDREN

1 In Canada and the United States, young adults are often encouraged to become quite independent. Their parents don't always tell them what to do. Work with a partner. Ask him or her the following questions.

Should parents tell their children:

1. what time to be home?
2. who to date?
3. what to study?
4. who to marry?
5. where to live?

2 Now present your answers to the class. What does most of the class think? Are there differences of opinion? Discuss the answers with your classmates.

PART TWO

◆ **TAKE A GUESS**

Sushila is talking to her friend Bob. Read these three sentences from their conversation. Then answer the question below. Discuss your answer with your classmates.

- ◆ "Has the game started?"
- ◆ "Those are good seats."
- ◆ "We'll get a great view of the ice from there."

Where are Sushila and Bob? Circle the correct answer.

a. at a movie theater

b. at a baseball game

c. at a hockey game

 HAVE YOU GOT IT?

Listen to the conversation. Read the two summaries below. Which summary describes the conversation? Check (✔) *A* or *B*.

☐ A. Sue and Bob go to a hockey game. They meet a classmate of Sue's. They agree to go to a movie together after the game.

☐ B. Sue and Bob go to a hockey game. They meet a classmate of Bob's. They agree to go to a restaurant together after the game.

 CHECK IT OUT

Listen again and answer the questions. Check (✔) *Sue*, *Bob*, or *Neil*. The first one is done for you.

	Sue	Bob	Neil
1. Who arrives late?	☐	✔	☐
2. Who is in Bob's math class?	☐	☐	☐
3. Who talks a lot about hockey?	☐	☐	☐
4. Who is from India?	☐	☐	☐
5. Whose parents are from Delhi?	☐	☐	☐

📼 DOUBLE-CHECK IT

Listen again. Read the questions. Circle the correct answers. The first
one is done for you.

1. How many minutes do Sue and Bob have to wait before   4   ⑤   10
   the game starts?
2. Which row are Bob and Sue sitting in?   4   14   40
3. Which pair of seats do they have?   5 and 6   6 and 7   7 and 8
4. How many hockey games has Neil been to before?   0   1   2
5. How many months has Neil been in North America?   8   18   80

◆ WORK IT OUT

Bob introduced Sue and Neil. What did they say? Circle the correct
phrases. The first one is done for you.

Bob: Sue, this is Neil.

1. **Sue:** (Hi)/Mm.
         ‾‾‾‾
         a. b.

2. **Bob:** Neil, this is/she's Sue.
                   ‾‾‾‾‾‾‾‾‾‾
                   a.   b.

3. **Neil:** Hi. You look wonderful/Nice to meet you, Sue.
                 ‾‾‾‾‾‾‾‾‾‾‾‾‾‾‾‾‾‾‾‾‾‾‾‾‾‾‾‾‾‾‾‾‾‾
                       a.   b.

4. **Sue:** Nice to meet you, too./I'm pleased to make your acquaintance.
            ‾‾
                      a.   b.

◆ ACT IT OUT

Work in groups of three. Take turns introducing the other two people
in your group. Include some information about the person you are
introducing.

◆ LET'S TALK ABOUT . . . SPORTS

In Canada and the United States, people often like to play and watch sports. The most popular sports are baseball, football, basketball, and hockey. Ask three classmates from different countries about sports. Complete the chart below. Begin like this:

Where are you from?
What's the most popular sport in your country?

Compare your chart with the charts of other classmates. What are the most popular sports?

	Example	1	2	3
Student's name	*Hans*			
Country	*Germany*			
The most popular sport in your country	*Soccer*			
Your favorite sport to watch	*Tennis*			
Your favorite sport to play	*Golf*			

Now work with a partner. Tell him or her about the most exciting game you have played or watched.

PART THREE

◆ TAKE A GUESS

Look at the picture. Then discuss the questions with your classmates.

1. Where are Bob, Sue, and Neil?
2. What are they talking about?

HAVE YOU GOT IT?

Listen to the conversation. Complete the sentences with words from the box. The first one is done for you.

park	university	restaurant
game	library	movie

Bob, Sue, and Neil:

1. are students at a *university* .

2. thought the _____ was exciting.

3. went to a _____ after the game.

4. will go to a _____ next Saturday.

📼 CHECK IT OUT

Listen again. Are these sentences correct? Check (✔) *Yes* or *No*. If *No*, correct the sentence. The first one is done for you.

	Yes	No

1. Sue is studying ~~engineering~~ *chemistry*. ☐ ☑

2. Neil is studying engineering. ☐ ☐

3. Bob has a student visa. ☐ ☐

4. Neil studies very hard. ☐ ☐

5. Neil will return to India in three months. ☐ ☐

📼 DOUBLE-CHECK IT

Listen again and answer the questions. Check (✔) *Sue*, *Bob*, or *Neil*. The first one is done for you.

	Sue	Bob	Neil
1. Who misses his or her family?	☐	☐	☑
2. Who pays the bill?	☐	☐	☐
3. Who paid the bill last time?	☐	☐	☐
4. Who will call Bob about the movie?	☐	☐	☐

◆ BODY LANGUAGE

1. Look at the picture in *Take a Guess* on page 7. Bob's thumb is up. What does this mean? Circle the correct answer.

   a. Here's the bill.

   b. The game was great! We won!

   c. Waiter, could I have more coffee?

2. Discuss these questions with your classmates.

   a. Does this gesture mean the same in your culture?
   b. If not, what gesture would you use? Show your classmates.

◆ WORK IT OUT

Read this article from the sports section of the newspaper. Complete the sentences with words from the box. The first one is done for you.

score	game	season	goal
team	lose	win	

GOLDEN EAGLES WIN AGAIN!

The Golden Eagles beat the Diablos again last night. This is their third victory this _____season_____. It was an exciting _____ with an incredible _____ of 5 to 1. The _____ has been playing very well this season, and they expect to _____ the game next weekend against the Miracle Sticks.

◆ IN OTHER WORDS

1 Read the conversations. What do the underlined words mean? Circle *a* or *b*. The first one is done for you.

1. **Bob:** Neil's a <u>bookworm</u>.

   a. a person who reads books about worms

   (b.) a person who reads a lot of books

2. **Sue:** You must miss your <u>folks</u>.

   a. parents

   b. friends

3. **Neil:** I'll have to go back to India.

   Sue: <u>How come</u>?

   a. Can I come?

   b. Why?

4. **Neil:** <u>You bet</u>!

   a. That's right!

   b. Make a bet!

5. **Sue:** Would you like to <u>join us</u>?

   a. jog with us

   b. come with us

2 What do you know about your classmates? Ask questions and find out:

- who is a <u>bookworm</u>.
- who lives with his or her <u>folks</u>.
- <u>how come</u> your classmate came to this class.
- who would like to <u>join you</u> for pizza.
- who would answer "<u>You bet!</u>" to the question "Do you want to go to a movie?"

◆ ACT IT OUT

Work with a partner. Choose a role and role-play the following situation. Then change roles.

Student A: Think of places you like to go to on weekends. Invite Student B to go somewhere with you this weekend.

Student B: Accept or turn down Student A's invitation.

Begin like this:

Student A: My friends and I are going to the movies next Saturday. Would you like to join us?

Student B: Yeah, I'd like that. What are you going to see?
or
I'm sorry, I can't. I'm busy on Saturday.

◆ LET'S TALK ABOUT . . . PAYING FOR MEALS

In Canada and the United States, when friends go to a restaurant, they often share the bill or take turns paying. What about in your culture? Discuss the following questions with a partner. Check the appropriate boxes.

1 Who pays the bill when friends go out?

	Your Answer	**Your Partner's Answer**
Everyone shares the bill.		
Everyone pays for his or her own meal.		
Everyone takes turn paying the bill.		

2 If one person pays for the bill, who does? Why?

	Your Answer	Your Partner's Answer
The man		
The woman		
The older		
The younger		
The richer		
Other _____		

Getting the Message

EPISODE TWO

PART ONE

◆ THINK BACK

Read these sentences about Episode One. Check (✔) what you know about the story. Put an X next to the information you don't know. The first one is done for you.

1. ✔ People have marriages of convenience to stay in the country.

2. _____ Sue's parents want a marriage of convenience for her.

3. _____ Sue doesn't like to be treated like a child.

4. _____ Sue and Bob have known each other since childhood.

5. _____ Sue and Bob met Neil at a hockey game.

6. _____ Neil is a foreign student from India.

7. _____ Sue, Bob, and Neil will see the movie *Rocky VII*.

HAVE YOU GOT IT?

Listen to the conversation. Answer the questions. Check (✔) *Sue* or *Neil*. The first one is done for you.

	Neil	Sue
1. Who will do three assignments for one class?	☐	✔
2. Who is very good-looking?	☐	☐
3. Who wants the best grades?	☐	☐
4. Who will have an arranged marriage?	☐	☐

CHECK IT OUT

Listen again. Read the questions and write *Yes* or *No*. The first one is done for you.

1. Does Sue want to see Neil again?   *yes*

2. Does Pat think Neil will have time for Sue? _____

3. Have Sue's parents found a husband for her? _____

4. Does Pat think Sue should enjoy herself? _____

 DOUBLE-CHECK IT

Listen again. Sue describes Neil. What does she talk about? Circle the correct letters on the picture.

a. hair
b. eyebrows
c. eyes
d. nose
e. ears
f. moustache
g. mouth

◆ **WORK IT OUT**

Pat wants to meet someone too. She put a personal ad in the student newspaper. Read Pat's ad. Then answer the questions below. Circle the correct answers.

Call Jerry 631-4771.

Good-looking female student, 23 years old, fun, interesting, is looking for handsome, intelligent, same age male for happy times! Call Pat 631-8294.

Good-looking SWM 20

1. What does Pat say about herself?

   a. She's attractive.

   b. She's intelligent.

   c. She's rich.

2. How old is the person Pat wants to meet?

   a. eighteen

   b. twenty-three

   c. twenty-nine

◆ **WHAT ABOUT YOU?**

Work with a partner. Discuss your answers to these questions.

1. What do you think about meeting people through a personal ad?
2. Would you answer a personal ad?
3. Would you write a personal ad for yourself?
4. How would you describe yourself in a personal ad?
5. What are other ways of meeting people?

◆ **ACT IT OUT**

Work with a partner. Take turns describing a person in the class. Your partner will guess who you are describing. Use the model below.

Student A: Well, she's/he's [tall, short, medium height]. She/He has [brown, blue, green, hazel] eyes. She's/He's [attractive, interesting, nice-looking]. She/He has [curly, straight, long, short, medium-length, black, brown, blonde, red] hair. And she's/he's [thin, medium weight, heavy]. [He has a moustache, beard.]

Student B: Oh, you mean the teacher?

◆ LET'S TALK ABOUT . . . ARRANGED MARRIAGES

1 In some countries, parents arrange marriages for their children. Parents decide who their children will marry. In Canada and the United States, children choose who they will marry. Work with your classmates. List the countries you are from. Next to each country, check (✔) if parents arrange marriages, if children decide, if both parents and children decide, or if other people decide.

Countries	Parents	Children	Both	Other
_____	☐	☐	☐	☐
_____	☐	☐	☐	☐
_____	☐	☐	☐	☐
_____	☐	☐	☐	☐
_____	☐	☐	☐	☐
_____	☐	☐	☐	☐

2 Look at the list. What is the most common way to decide on marriage? Which way do you prefer? Discuss your answers with your classmates.

PART TWO

◆ TAKE A GUESS

Read the words below. What do you think the conversation will be about? Discuss your answer with your classmates.

phone	Neil	message	Mrs. Chopra	movie

HAVE YOU GOT IT?

Listen to the conversation. Why is Neil calling? Circle your answer.

a. to talk to Mrs. Chopra

b. to leave a message for Sue

c. to invite Sue to a movie

📼 CHECK IT OUT

Listen again and complete the note. The first one is done for you.

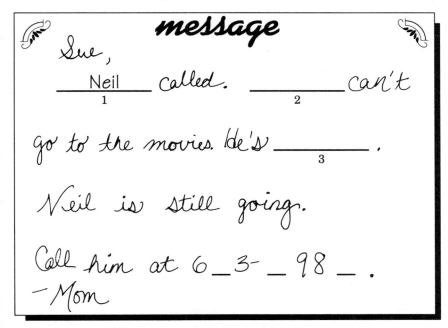

message

Sue,

_____Neil_____ called. _____ can't
      1   2

go to the movies. He's _____ .
                                 3

Neil is still going.

Call him at 6_3-_98_ .
— Mom

◆ BETWEEN THE LINES

Read the questions. Circle your answers. Then discuss your answers
with your classmates.

1. How does Mrs. Chopra feel?

   a. tired

   b. angry

2. How does Neil sound?

   a. frightened

   b. excited

3. How is Neil's behavior?

   a. rude

   b. polite

◆ WORK IT OUT

Mrs. Chopra took Neil's message. Put these sentences from their
conversation in the correct order. Number the sentences from 1 to 6.
The first one is done for you.

a. _____ **Mrs. Chopra:** No, she isn't.

b. _____ **Neil:** Please tell her Neil called.

c. __1__ **Mrs. Chopra:** Hello.

d. _____ **Neil:** Oh, um, well, can I leave a message?

e. _____ **Mrs. Chopra:** Go ahead.

f. _____ **Neil:** Hello. Is Sue there, please?

Work with a partner. Take turns leaving a message. Use Mrs. Chopra and Neil's conversation in *Work It Out* as a model.

   ➤ **Student A:** Call Student B on the telephone. Leave a message for your friend to call you.

   ➤ **Student B:** Answer the call and take a message.

◆ LET'S TALK ABOUT . . . TELEPHONE ETIQUETTE

In Canada and the United States, there are certain social rules for telephoning. Look at the telephone etiquette list. Are the rules the same or different in your culture? Discuss the rules with your classmates.

Telephone Etiquette:

1. When you answer a phone call, say "Hello" first.

2. When you make a phone call, identify yourself.

3. If you take a message, repeat it to make sure it's correct.

4. Before you hang up, say "Good-bye."

5. Except for emergencies, don't call after 11:00 P.M. or before 8:00 A.M.

6. Other _____

PART THREE

◆ TAKE A GUESS

Look at the picture. Then discuss these questions on the next page with your classmates.

1. How does Mrs. Chopra look?
2. How does Sushila look?
3. What does Mrs. Chopra have in her hand?
4. What do you think they are talking about?

📼 HAVE YOU GOT IT?

Listen to the conversation. Read the summary and correct the mistakes.
The first one is done for you.

Mrs. Chopra and Sushila are arguing. Mrs. Chopra is angry about ~~Bob~~ *Neil*

and Sushila going to the hockey game. Sushila is happy because she is

allowed to do what she wants.

📼 CHECK IT OUT

Listen again. Are these sentences correct? Check (✔) *Yes* or *No*. If *No*,
correct the sentence. The first one is done for you.

	Yes	No
1. Sushila ~~can~~ *can't* go out with boys her parents don't know.	☐	✔
2. Sushila can go out with Bob.	☐	☐
3. Sushila can choose her girlfriends.	☐	☐
4. Sushila can choose her boyfriends.	☐	☐
5. Sushila can see her friends at school.	☐	☐

📼 DOUBLE-CHECK IT

Listen again. Put the sentences in the correct order. Number them
from 1 to 3.

Sushila says:

_____ a. she wants to be friends with Neil.

_____ b. Neil is Bob's friend.

_____ c. she is old enough to choose her friends.

Complete the sentences. Circle *a, b,* or *c.* Then discuss your answers in small groups.

1. Sushila thinks her mother is:
   a. fair.
   b. too old.
   c. too strict.

2. Sushila thinks she doesn't have enough:
   a. friends.
   b. freedom.
   c. money.

◆ **WHAT DO YOU THINK?**

Mrs. Chopra gives Sushila rules she must follow. Do you agree or disagree with the rules? Check (✔) your answer. Then discuss your reasons with your classmates.

Rules	Agree	Disagree
1. Sushila can only go out with boys her parents know.	☐	☐
2. Sushila can go out with Bob.	☐	☐
3. Sushila can choose her girlfriends.	☐	☐
4. Sushila can't choose her boyfriends.	☐	☐
5. Sushila can see the friends her parents don't know only at school.	☐	☐

◆ **IN OTHER WORDS**

1 Read the conversations. What do the underlined words mean? For each conversation, choose the correct answer from the list and write it in the blank.

   ◆ unreasonable
   ◆ you don't have another choice
   ◆ become friends with

   a. **Sushila:** But, Mom, I just met him. I don't even know him.

   Mrs. Chopra: Well, then why are you going to a movie with him?

   Sushila: So I can get to know him!

   _____

b. **Sushila:** Mom, please! Let me choose my own friends.

Mrs. Chopra: Girlfriends only! Not boys!

Sushila: But, Mom, I'm twenty-one years old. This is <u>ridiculous</u>.

Mrs. Chopra: Ridiculous!? Why is it so ridiculous?

Sushila: Because other people my age choose their own friends. Why can't I?

_____

c. **Mrs. Chopra:** If your father and I don't know your friends, then you can see them at school only.

Sushila: Well, it's not fair.

Mrs. Chopra: Maybe not. But <u>that's how it is</u>.

_____

2 Work with a partner. Discuss your answers to these questions.

a. Think of a famous person you would like to get to know. Why did you choose that person?

b. You are waiting to pay for a carton of milk. You are in line. There's only one cashier. There are fifteen people ahead of you. Why is this situation ridiculous? Think of a ridiculous situation you were in last week. What was it? Why was it ridiculous?

c. Your boss really needs you to work on the weekends. You don't want to because you have a family. But he says, "That's how it is." What would you say? Can you think of another choice, for example, working only one weekend a month?

◆ BODY LANGUAGE

1 Look at the picture in _Take a Guess_ on page 16. Sushila's hands are on her hips and her eyes are rolled up. What does this mean? Circle the correct answers. (There is more than one correct answer.)

a. She is frustrated.

b. She is angry.

c. She wants to dance.

d. She doesn't like what she is hearing.

e. Her pants are too tight.

2 Discuss these questions with your classmates.

a. Does this gesture mean the same in your culture?

b. If not, what gesture would you use? Show your classmates.

◆ LET'S TALK ABOUT...DATING

1 In Canada and the United States, people often start dating (meeting a boy or girl socially) in their teens. On a date, people may go to parties, movies, dances, or sports events. Work in small groups. Ask each other these questions and fill in the chart.

1. What country are you from?
2. Do people date in that country?
3. At what age do people start dating?
4. Where do they go?
5. Do they go out in a group, in couples, or with parents?

Countries	Do You Date?	At What Age?	Where Do You Go?	Do You Go in Groups, in Couples, or with Parents?

2 Look at the chart. Discuss the answers with your classmates. Is dating different from culture to culture? If yes, what are the differences? Why do you think there are differences?

Jealousy Strikes

PART ONE

THINK BACK

What happened in Episode Two? Read these sentences. Write *T* if the sentence is true. Write *F* if the sentence is false. Correct the false sentences. The first one is done for you.

1. __F__ Sue tells Pat that she is ~~not~~ interested in Neil.

2. _____ Sue and Pat talk about the marriage her parents are arranging for her.

3. _____ Neil speaks to Sue's father on the phone.

4. _____ Neil says he can't go to the movie.

5. _____ Sue's mother is angry because Sue is going out with Neil.

TAKE A GUESS

Sue and Neil are going somewhere together. Where do you think they are going? Discuss your answer with your classmates.

HAVE YOU GOT IT?

Listen to the conversation. Read the entry in Sue's journal and correct the mistakes. The first one is done for you.

> I went out with ~~Bob~~ *Neil*. It was great. We walked through the park and then went to a coffee shop. We talked about all kinds of things. I apologized for my dad. Neil understood why she was happy about his call. He asked a lot of questions about Pat. I don't know why.

Listen again and answer the questions. Circle *a* or *b*. The first one is done for you.

1. When will the movie start?

   a. in an hour

   ⓑ in half an hour

2. Where do Sue and Neil go before the movie?

   a. to a park

   b. to a coffee shop

3. Who is really fun?

   a. Bob

   b. Neil

4. How long has Sue known Bob?

   a. a short time

   b. a long time

5. Why is Neil always busy?

   a. he's studying

   b. he's working

DOUBLE-CHECK IT

Listen again. How often do people do things? Check (✔) the correct box. The first one is done for you.

How often:	Never	Rarely	Sometimes	Often	Always
1. has Sue's mother met Neil?	✔	☐	☐	☐	☐
2. does Sue's mother want to know where she is?	☐	☐	☐	☐	☐
3. do Bob and Sue go to hockey games?	☐	☐	☐	☐	☐
4. do Bob and Sue go out with friends?	☐	☐	☐	☐	☐
5. does Neil go out?	☐	☐	☐	☐	☐

◆ WHAT ABOUT YOU?

Work with a partner. Ask your partner these questions and write the answers. Use *never, rarely, sometimes, often,* or *always.*

How often do you:

1. read a book in English? _____

2. talk on the phone in English? _____

3. watch a movie in English? _____

4. meet with native English speakers? _____

5. write a letter in English? _____

◆ BETWEEN THE LINES

Read these questions. Discuss your answers with your classmates.

1. Is Sue happy that her mother wants to know where she is, who she is with, and when she will be home? Why or why not?

2. Does Neil think it's okay that Sue's mother wants to know this? Why or why not?

◆ WHAT DO YOU THINK?

Answer these questions. Circle *a* or *b*. Then discuss with your classmates the reasons for your opinions.

1. Why does Neil ask Sue about Bob?

   a. He likes Bob.

   b. He thinks Sue and Bob may be dating.

2. Do you think Sue and Bob are dating?

   a. Yes

   b. No

PART TWO

◆ TAKE A GUESS

Look at the picture and discuss these questions with your classmates.

1. What is happening?

2. Neil tells his friend Dan about his problem. What problem do you think Neil has?

🔊 HAVE YOU GOT IT?

Listen to the conversation. Read the question and circle the best answer.

What is Neil's problem?

a. His class is very difficult.

b. He doesn't like Bob.

c. He isn't sure about Bob and Sue's friendship.

d. He's unhappy because he has no friends.

📼 CHECK IT OUT

Listen again. What does Dan tell Neil? Check (✔) your answers.

Dan tells Neil:

a. ☐ that men and women can be friends.

b. ☐ that Bob and Sue are dating.

c. ☐ that men and women often go out together.

d. ☐ to ask Sue for a date.

e. ☐ to ask Sue about Bob.

f. ☐ to tell Sue she is beautiful.

◆ BETWEEN THE LINES

Read the questions. Circle your answers. Discuss your answers with your classmates.

1. Why is Neil unsure about asking Sue out?

   a. He is too shy.

   b. He isn't very interested in her.

   c. He thinks she's dating Bob.

2. Why does Neil say "See what I mean?" when he sees Sue and Bob hugging?

   a. He's embarrassed.

   b. He thinks this means Sue and Bob are dating.

   c. He thinks Sue doesn't like him.

◆ WHAT DO YOU THINK?

Work with a partner. Discuss your answers to these questions.

1. Dan advised Neil to ask Sue for a date. Do you agree with this advice?
2. What advice would you give Neil?

◆ ACT IT OUT

Work with a partner. Choose a role and role-play the following situation. Then change roles.

◈ **Student A:** You can't understand what your teacher is saying in your English class. Ask Student B for advice.

◈ **Student B:** Student A tells you his or her problem. Give him or her advice.

Begin like this:

Student A: I can't understand my English teacher. What should I do?

Student B: Why don't you...   or If I were you, I would...   or   You could...

This letter is from a newspaper advice column. Read the letter. Then answer the questions.

Advice

Dear Maggie,
I am a new immigrant to this country. I've been here only three months, but I'm wondering if I made a mistake coming here. I can't find a job, I have no friends, and I miss my family. I feel very alone and unhappy. What can I do?

Lost in Notown

1. What are "Lost in Notown's" problems? Circle your answers. She's

   a. lonely

   b. frightened

   c. unemployed

   d. sick

   e. sad

2. What advice would you give her?

3. Do you have advice columns in your country?

4. Would you take the advice of a newspaper writer? Why or why not?

5. Where else can you get advice?

◆ **BODY LANGUAGE**

Look at the picture in *Take a Guess* on page 24. Bob and Sue are hugging. Hugging can have different purposes. Some are listed below. Check (✔) the purposes hugging has in your culture.

Hugging is used to:

1. say hello. ☐

2. say good-bye. ☐

3. congratulate someone. ☐

4. comfort someone. ☐

5. show someone you like him or her. ☐

6. other _____ ☐

◆ LET'S TALK ABOUT ... GREETINGS

1 People from different cultures have different ways of greeting someone or saying "hello." In Canada and the United States, people shake hands with someone they don't know and as a form of greeting in business situations. Family and close friends may hug and kiss one another. What types of greeting do you use in the culture you come from? Do you greet strangers, friends, family, and business associates differently? Discuss this with your classmates and complete the chart below.

Country	Greeting Used with Strangers	Greeting Used with Friends	Greeting Used with Family	Greeting Used in Business

2 Discuss these questions with your classmates.

  a. Are there some greetings that are the same in all cultures?
  b. Are there any greetings that would make you feel uncomfortable?
  c. Are there special words used for greeting different people?

PART THREE ~~~~~~~~~~~~~~

 HAVE YOU GOT IT?

Listen to the conversation. Read the question and circle the best answer.

Why does Sue call Neil?

a. to ask him if he's feeling okay

b. to invite him to an exhibition

c. to ask him about an assignment

◆ 27 ◆

CHECK IT OUT

Listen again. Neil wrote himself a note. Which is the correct note?
Check (✔) *A* or *B*.

A. ☐   B. ☐

DID YOU GET THAT?

Listen again. Neil and Sue make some suggestions. How do they
respond to these suggestions? Match the suggestions with the correct
responses. Write a letter from Column B next to each suggestion in
Column A.

A. Suggestion

1. How about getting there before the crowds? ____

2. Let's meet somewhere near the gallery. ____

3. Why don't we meet inside then? ____

B. Response

a. Yeah, that's fine.
b. Sure.
c. Okay.
d. Good idea.
e. All right.

◆ ACT IT OUT

Work with a partner. Choose a role and role-play the following
situation. Use the expressions in *Did You Get That?* Then change
roles.

Student A: Make a suggestion to Student B about where to go for
lunch.

Student B: Respond to Student A's suggestion. Suggest what time
to meet.

Student A: Respond to Student B's suggestion.

◆ BETWEEN THE LINES

Read the questions. Circle your answers. Then discuss your answers
with your classmates.

1. How does Neil sound when he is
   talking to Sue on the telephone?

   a. friendly

   b. unfriendly

   c. excited

2. Why does Neil sound this way?

   a. He's happy Sue is inviting him out.

   b. He's upset because he saw Sue and
      Bob hugging.

   c. He's tired because he's studying
      hard.

◆ LET'S TALK ABOUT...MEN AND WOMEN

1 Sue called Neil and invited him out. In Canada and the United
States, it's okay for a woman to do this. Look at the chart. In some
cultures, only men do these things; in other cultures, it's okay only
for women; in others, it's okay for men and women. Think about the
culture you come from and check (✔) who usually does these things.
Then compare your answers with a partner's.

Who:	Women	Men	Women and Men
invites someone on a date?			
walks through a door first?			
pays when a couple is on a date?			
orders the food at a restaurant?			
helps someone with his or her coat?			

2 Discuss these questions with your classmates.

   a. Are there other things that only women or only men can do?

   b. What happens if someone doesn't follow these "rules"?

Close Encounter

EPISODE FOUR

PART ONE

◆ THINK BACK

What happened in Episode Three? Answer the questions. Circle *a* or *b*.

1. Who did Neil ask for advice on relationships?
   a. Dan
   b. Sue

2. Who was upset when he saw Sue hugging Bob?
   a. Neil
   b. Dan

3. Who did Sue invite to the art gallery?
   a. Bob
   b. Neil

◆ TAKE A GUESS

Read these three sentences from the conversation. Then answer the questions below. Discuss your answers with your classmates.

◆ "Neil, is something wrong?"

◆ "Well, I saw you and Bob at school."

◆ "We're just friends."

1. Who is speaking?

   _____

2. What do you think they are talking about?

   _____

📼 HAVE YOU GOT IT?

Listen to the conversation. What is the conversation about? Circle the correct answer.

a. Neil doesn't want to see Sue.

b. Sue doesn't want to be friends with Bob.

c. Neil doesn't understand why Sue and Bob hugged.

📼 CHECK IT OUT

Listen again. Read these sentences. Write *T* if the sentence is true. Write *F* if the sentence is false. Correct the false sentences.

1. _____ Sue and Neil are at the art gallery.

2. _____ Sue tells Neil she is Bob's girlfriend.

3. _____ Sue tells Neil she's sorry about the misunderstanding.

📼 DOUBLE-CHECK IT

Listen again. Complete the sentences. Circle *a, b,* or *c.*

1. Sue hugged Bob to:

   a. say hello.

   b. comfort him.

   c. congratulate him.

2. The news Bob got was that:

   a. he won the lottery.

   b. his sister had a baby.

   c. he passed an important exam.

◆ IN OTHER WORDS

Read the conversations. What do the underlined sentences mean? Circle *a* or *b.*

1. **Sue:** Yeah, and you sounded strange on the phone, too. <u>What's going on?</u>

   Neil: Well, actually, I, I . . .

   Sue: Yes. Tell me. Did something happen?

   a. What's happening?

   b. Where are you going?

2. **Sue:** Oh, Neil! <u>I get it!</u> No! We're just friends. Don't worry about Bob and me.

   a. I want it.

   b. I understand.

3. **Sue:** <u>There's nothing between us.</u>

   Neil: There isn't?

   Sue: No. I'm not Bob's girlfriend.

   a. We're not dating.

   b. We don't like each other very much.

◆ WHAT ABOUT YOU?

1 Work with a partner. Read each situation. Answer the questions.
Write *Yes* or *No*.

Situations	Your Answer	Your Partner's Answer
1. Your girlfriend/boyfriend/spouse dances most of the evening with another partner. Are you jealous?		
2. You see your girlfriend/boyfriend/spouse in a restaurant with a handsome man/beautiful woman. Are you jealous?		
3. Your parents gave your sister a two-week paid vacation for her birthday. On your birthday, they give you a pen. Are you jealous?		
4. Your rich uncle died. He left your brother a lot of money. He left you his beat-up, old car. Are you jealous?		

2 Compare your answers with your partner's. Discuss why you are or
are not jealous.

◆ LET'S TALK ABOUT...EXPRESSING EMOTIONS

In each culture, people express their emotions differently. Read the
following two situations on page 33. For each one, choose the picture
below that shows how you would feel and write the number of the
situation below the picture. Then circle what you would do in the
situation. Discuss your answers with a partner.

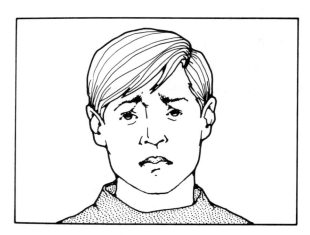
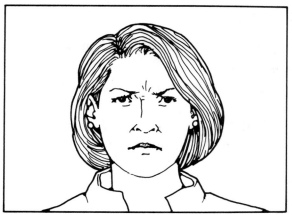

Situation One

Your best friend has just told you that his or her mother or father died. You:

a. say, "I'm really sorry."

b. put your arm around his or her shoulder and say, "I'm sorry."

c. start to cry, and hug your friend.

d. other _____

Situation Two

You and your husband or wife have tickets for a concert. Your husband or wife came home many hours after he or she was supposed to come home. Now, it's too late to go to the concert. You:

a. say, "Dear, why are you so late?"

b. shout and ask for an explanation.

c. scream, leave the house, and slam the door behind you.

d. other _____

Part Two 〰〰〰〰〰〰〰〰〰〰

◆ TAKE A GUESS

Use the clues to solve the riddle. Write the answers to the clues in the blanks.

Clues:

1. what you see in an art gallery
2. who Sue met at the hockey game with Bob

Sue and Neil talk about _____ and _____'s future.
                                            1   2

📼 HAVE YOU GOT IT?

Listen to the conversation. What are Sue and Neil talking about?
Check (✔) the topics.

a. ☐ homework

b. ☐ paintings

c. ☐ staying in the country

d. ☐ sculptures

e. ☐ going to another university

◆ 33 ◆

Listen again. Sue makes three suggestions to Neil. Circle the reasons her suggestions are not possible.

Sue's Suggestions	Reasons
1. Extend his student visa	a. Neil's parents don't have much money. b. Neil doesn't want to take any more courses.
2. Find work at the university	a. University jobs are boring. b. Lots of people want a job.
3. Have a marriage of convenience	a. Sue wasn't serious. b. No one wants to marry Neil.

DOUBLE-CHECK IT

Listen again. After they see Exhibit A, where do Sue and Neil go in the art gallery? Look at the art gallery floor plan. Draw Sue and Neil's path from Exhibit A to the next exhibit they see.

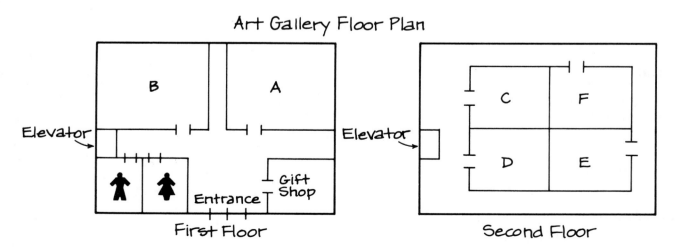

Art Gallery Floor Plan

◆ IN OTHER WORDS

Read the conversations. What do the underlined sentences mean?
Circle *a* or *b*.

1. **Neil:** Well, I don't think my parents have enough money to pay for any more courses.

   Sue: Oh, I see. <u>That's too bad.</u> Well, can you work? Maybe get a job at the university?

   a. That's unfortunate.

   b. That's unacceptable.

2. **Neil:** <u>It's hard.</u> Lots of people apply for work.

   a. It's impossible.

   b. It's difficult.

3. **Sue:** Neil! <u>I was only kidding!</u>

   a. I was making a joke.

   b. I was thinking of children.

◆ BETWEEN THE LINES

Read the sentences. Circle your answers. Then discuss your answers
with your classmates.

1. Sue makes suggestions to Neil about staying in the country because she:

   a. likes Neil a lot and wants him to stay.

   b. thinks his education is very important.

2. Sue wasn't serious about the marriage of convenience suggestion because she:

   a. thinks marriages of convenience are wrong.

   b. doesn't want to get married.

◆ ACT IT OUT

Work with a partner. Choose a role and role-play the following
situation. Then change roles.

◆ **Student A:** Tell Student B how to get from your classroom to one of these places: the restroom or the cafeteria.

◆ **Student B:** Listen to Student A's directions. Then tell Student A how to get from your classroom to one of these places: the cafeteria or the bus stop.

Begin like this:

Student A: When you leave the classroom, turn left/turn right/go straight.

◆ WHAT DO YOU THINK?

Neil talks to Sue about what he wants to do in the future. What do you think he should do? Work with a partner, using the list of suggestions to help you. Write your suggestions in the blank.

Neil should _____

_____

Possible suggestions:

◆ go back home and work
◆ go to a university in India
◆ apply for immigrant status
◆ try hard to get a job at the university
◆ try to get a job at another university
◆ other _____

◆ LET'S TALK ABOUT ... EDUCATION

1 In Canada and the United States, many young people pay for their university education. In some other cultures, university education is paid for by the government. Some young people go to a university after high school, but sometimes they go later in life, when they are in their thirties or forties. What about in the culture you come from? Work with a partner and complete the chart below.

	Country	Who Pays for Education?	Age When Most People Go to a University
You			
Your partner			

2 Discuss these questions with your classmates.

   a. Should university studies be free for everyone?
   b. What is the best age to go to a university? Why?

PART THREE

◆ TAKE A GUESS

Look at the picture. Read the questions. Then circle *a* or *b*.

1. How do you think Sushila feels?

   a. shocked

   b. in pain

2. How do you think Mrs. Chopra feels?

   a. angry

   b. worried

3. What do you think will happen next?

   a. Sushila and Neil will take Mrs. Chopra to the art gallery.

   b. Sushila and Mrs. Chopra will argue about something.

📼 HAVE YOU GOT IT?

Listen to the conversation. Were your answers to *Take a Guess* correct?
If not, discuss the corrections.

CHECK IT OUT

Listen again. Are these sentences correct? Check (✔) *Yes* or *No*. If *No*, correct the sentence.

	Yes	No
1. Neil and Sushila decide to go for coffee.	☐	☐
2. Sushila introduces Neil to her mother.	☐	☐
3. Neil knows his way home.	☐	☐
4. Sushila and Neil leave together.	☐	☐

DOUBLE-CHECK IT

Listen again and answer the questions. Check (✔) *Mrs. Chopra*, *Sushila*, or *Neil*.

	Mrs. Chopra	Sushila	Neil
1. Who thanks someone?	☐	☐	☐
2. Who knows a nice place for coffee?	☐	☐	☐
3. Who invites Mrs. Chopra for coffee?	☐	☐	☐
4. Who won't argue on the street?	☐	☐	☐
5. Who apologizes to someone?	☐	☐	☐

◆ BETWEEN THE LINES

Complete the sentences. Circle your answers. Then discuss your answers with your classmates.

1. Mrs. Chopra is angry because:

   a. she doesn't want Sushila to have a boyfriend from India.

   b. Sushila did something she wasn't allowed to do.

2. Neil is nervous because he:

   a. knows Mrs. Chopra is angry.

   b. has to go home alone.

◆ WHAT DO YOU THINK?

Discuss these questions with your classmates.

1. Do you think Sushila and Neil will see each other again?
2. Why or why not?

◆ ACT IT OUT

Work with a partner. Choose a role and role-play the following situation. Then change roles.

➤ **Student A:** You invited Student B to go somewhere with you (to a restaurant for lunch, to a party, to a movie, to a museum). Say that you enjoyed it and ask about Student B.

◆ **Student B:** Respond to Student A's question, using an adjective such as *delicious*, *nice*, *good*, or *interesting*. Then thank him or her for inviting you.

◆ **Student A:** Accept Student B's thank you. Thank him or her for coming.

Begin like this:

Student A: I enjoyed the exhibit. How about you?

◆ LET'S TALK ABOUT...BAD MANNERS

Mrs. Chopra did not want to argue with her daughter on the street. In some cultures, it is considered bad manners to argue in public. Look at the chart. Think about the culture you come from, and answer the questions. Write *Yes* or *No*. Then compare your answer with your partner's. Add other behaviors that you think are bad manners.

Is it bad manners to:	Your Answer	Your Partner's Answer
1. argue in public?		
2. eat noisily?		
3. interrupt someone who is talking?		
4. not use please and thank you?		
5. spit in a public place?		
6. talk loudly to a classmate when the teacher is lecturing?		
7. talk loudly during a movie?		
8.		
9.		
10.		

Suspicious Hearts

PART ONE

◆ THINK BACK

What happened in Episode Four? Read the entry in Sue's journal. Put the letters of the underlined words in the correct order. The first one is done for you.

> NEIL
> Mom saw <u>ILNE</u> and me outside the gallery. She
> was really <u>GRANY</u>. Too bad! Neil and I
> had such a <u>DGOO</u> time there. I really <u>EKLI</u>
> him. I think he likes me, too. He was
> jealous of <u>BBO</u>.

◆ TAKE A GUESS

Look at the picture. Then discuss these questions with your classmates.

1. Where are Sue and Neil?
2. How does Sue look? Why?
3. How does Neil look? Why?

📼 HAVE YOU GOT IT?

Listen to the conversation. What are Sue and Neil talking about?
Check (✔) the topics.

a. ☐ Sue's argument with her mother

b. ☐ the food at the restaurant

c. ☐ finding work for Neil

d. ☐ tipping in restaurants

e. ☐ exams at the university

f. ☐ Sue's arranged marriage

📼 CHECK IT OUT

Listen again. Number the sentences in the correct order. The first one
is done for you.

_____ a. Neil says he can't find a job.

_1_ b. Sue tells Neil she is grounded.

_____ c. Neil pays the bill.

_____ d. Sue says her parents are looking for a husband for her.

_____ e. Sue and Neil say they want to continue going out.

🔊 DOUBLE-CHECK IT

Listen again. Match the questions with the correct numbers. The first one is done for you.

1. _e_ How many job applications are there?   a. 15

2. ___ How many jobs are there?   b. 2

3. ___ What percent of the bill is usually left as a tip?   c. 10

4. ___ How much are Sue and Neil's coffees?   d. $6.50

5. ___ How many pieces of cake did Sue and Neil have?   e. 200

6. ___ How much was the bill?   f. $1.50

◆ IN OTHER WORDS

Read the conversations. What do the underlined words mean? Circle *a* or *b*.

1. **Sue:** Well, I had a big argument with her, and now I'm grounded!

   Neil: Grounded? What do you mean?

   a. I have to walk everywhere.

   b. I can't go out.

2. **Sue:** I can handle that. I've been grounded before.

   a. I can pick it up.

   b. I can manage.

3. **Neil:** Well, he said there's no chance.

   Sue: Oh, no! That's too bad.

   a. It's not good enough.

   b. I'm sorry to hear that.

◆ LET'S TALK ABOUT . . . TIPPING

In restaurants in Canada and the United States, we usually leave a tip for the waiter or waitress. This extra money is for good service, and the customer leaves it on the table. Work with a partner. Discuss these questions.

1. Do you tip in the country you come from?
2. If you tip, do you tip waiters or waitresses, hair stylists, and taxi drivers?
3. What other people do you tip?
4. How much tip do you give them?
5. Is tipping a good idea, or should employers pay their employees more money?

PART TWO

◆ TAKE A GUESS

Use the clues to solve the riddle. Write the answers to the clues in the blanks.

Clues

1. Sue's friend since childhood
2. Sue's boyfriend
3. a word for mother and father

_____ and Sue talk about _____ and Sue's
　　　　1　　　　　　　　　　　　　　　　　　2

problem with her _____ .
　　　　　　　　　　　3

🔲 HAVE YOU GOT IT?

Listen to the conversation. Complete each sentence using a word from the box.

grounded	party	test	sick

1. Sue tells Bob about being _____ .

2. Bob is going to have a _____ .

🔲 CHECK IT OUT

Listen again. Are these sentences correct? Check (✔) *Yes* or *No*. If *No*, correct the sentence.

	Yes	No
1. Bob thinks Sue should be grounded.	☐	☐
2. Sue and Neil want to see each other again.	☐	☐
3. Sue loves her parents.	☐	☐
4. Sue says she will go to the party.	☐	☐
5. Sue wants to date other men.	☐	☐

Listen again. How do Sue and Bob feel? Circle your answers.

1. Sue feels upset/sad about being grounded.
2. Bob feels sorry/angry about Sue's situation.
3. Sue feels good/guilty about going to Bob's party.

◆ **IN OTHER WORDS**

Read the conversations. What do the underlined words mean? Circle *a* or *b*.

1. **Bob:** How are you doing?

   Sue: Oh, you know. Same old story.

   a. Nothing's different.

   b. I'm getting old.

2. **Bob:** Well, that's too bad 'cause I'm having a party Saturday night. And you're invited.

   Sue: Really!? Sounds good. What kind of party?

   a. Your voice is nice.

   b. That's a good idea.

3. **Bob:** Well, I've asked everybody to bring something to eat or drink, so . . .

   Sue: A potluck! Great!

   a. Each person will bring something to eat or drink.

   b. It will be a lucky party for everyone who goes.

4. **Sue:** My parents are already looking for a husband for me!

   Bob: Oh, so you're really stuck.

   a. in a difficult situation

   b. very lucky

◆ WORK IT OUT

Bob left a note in Sue's locker after they talked. Bob has terrible writing! Correct Bob's note by adding capital letters and periods. The first sentence is done for you.

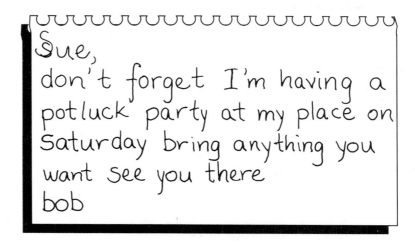

Sue,
don't forget I'm having a potluck party at my place on Saturday bring anything you want see you there
bob

◆ WHAT'S THE WORD?

Complete the crossword with words from the conversation. Number 3 is done for you.

Across

1. Mrs. Chopra's daughter
2. Sue's parents want to find this for Sue.
3. Bob gave Sue an

   _____ .

Down

4. Sue may be having one of these soon.
5. Sue's longtime friend
6. The kind of party Bob is having
7. Sue was punished. She was _____ .

◆ BETWEEN THE LINES

Read the questions. Circle your answers. Discuss your answers with your classmates.

1. Why does Sue feel guilty about going to Bob's party?

    a. She will have to lie to her parents.

    b. She can't bring any food to the party.

2. Why does Bob feel sorry for Sue?

    a. Sue won't know anyone at his party.

    b. He understands her feelings about Neil and her parents.

◆ WHAT DO YOU THINK?

Work with a partner. Discuss the questions. Give reasons for your opinions.

1. Should Sue be grounded?
2. Should Sue lie to her parents?
3. Should Sue see Neil again?

◆ WHAT ABOUT YOU?

Sue feels guilty lying to her parents. Read the following situations. How would you feel about lying in these situations? Check *Guilty* or *Not Guilty*. Discuss your answers with your classmates.

	Guilty	Not Guilty
1. Your classmate asks your opinion about his or her homework. The homework is very bad. You lie and say it's okay.		
2. Your five-year-old child wants to know where babies come from. You lie and say the stork (a bird) brings them.		
3. You oversleep. Your boss asks you why you are late for work. You lie and say your car broke down.		
4. Your friend invites you to his or her place for dinner. You don't like the food. You lie and say it's delicious.		

◆ LET'S TALK ABOUT ... DISCIPLINING TEENAGERS

1 In Canada and the United States, parents sometimes discipline their
teenage children for staying out late or disobeying rules. Examples
of discipline are grounding or no allowance (money parents give to
children). What about in the culture you come from? Complete the
chart with your class.

Country	Are Teenagers Disciplined?	What Are They Disciplined For?	Examples of Discipline

2 Do you think parents should be very strict with their children or
give their children a lot of freedom? Why or why not?

PART THREE

◆ TAKE A GUESS

Look at the picture. Then discuss these questions with your classmates.

1. Where are the people?
2. Who do you think they are?
3. What are they doing?

📼 HAVE YOU GOT IT?

Listen to the conversation. Sue overhears two people talking. What is their conversation about? Circle the correct answer.

a. the difficulty of finding a good husband

b. a marriage of convenience

c. talking in the library

Listen again. Answer the questions. Check (✔) *Yes* or *No*.

	Yes	No
1. Is the guy in Dan's class?	☐	☐
2. Is the guy going to ask the girl to marry him?	☐	☐
3. Does the guy love the girl?	☐	☐
4. Does the girl think the guy loves her?	☐	☐

🖭 **DOUBLE-CHECK IT**

Listen again. What is Liz's opinion? Circle the correct answers. There is more than one correct answer.

a. Someone should call Immigration.

b. Someone should tell the girl about the guy's plan.

c. Dan should talk to the guy.

d. Liz should talk to the girl.

◆ **WHAT DO YOU THINK?**

Work with a partner. Discuss these questions.

1. Do you think Liz and Dan are talking about Sue and Neil?
2. Why or why not?

◆ **BODY LANGUAGE**

1 Look at the picture in *Take a Guess* on page 48. The student standing has her finger over her mouth. What does this mean? Circle the correct answer.

a. Study!

b. Be quiet!

c. My mouth hurts!

d. Leave the room!

2 Discuss these questions with your classmates.

a. Does this gesture mean the same in the culture you're from?
b. If not, what gesture would you use? Show your classmates.

◆ LET'S TALK ABOUT...SSHHH!

1 In Canada and the United States, certain places are usually
  very quiet (for example, libraries, churches, and theaters during
  performances). Work with a partner. Make lists of places that are
  usually quiet in the culture you come from.

You	Your Partner

2 Discuss your list with your classmates. Are your lists the same?
  How are they different? Do some cultures have more quiet places
  than other cultures?

Marry Me!

PART ONE

THINK BACK

What happened in Episode Five? Read these statements from Episode Five. Who said them? Write *Bob*, *Sue*, *Neil*, or *Dan*. The first one is done for you.

1. "And my parents are starting to look for a husband for me!" — *Sue*

2. "Well, I talked to someone about a job here." _____

3. "I'm having a party Saturday night." _____

4. "And he's going to ask her to marry him!" _____

TAKE A GUESS

Sue goes to Bob's party. What do you think will happen? Circle the correct answer.

a. Sue will see Neil.

b. Mrs. Chopra will arrive at the party.

c. Sue and Neil will argue.

HAVE YOU GOT IT?

Listen to the conversation. What happens? Check (✔) the correct answers.

a. ☐ Sue arrives late at Bob's party.

b. ☐ Sue is upset that Neil isn't at the party.

c. ☐ Sue is happy to see Neil because she hasn't seen him in the last few days.

d. ☐ Sue meets Dan.

Listen again. What do Bob, Neil, Sue, and Dan say? Look at the picture below and fill in the missing words in their conversations.

🎙 <u>**DID YOU GET THAT?**</u>

Listen again. Bob is the host of the party, so he asks people what they would like to eat and drink. How do they answer? Circle *a* or *b*.

1. **Bob:** Can I get you a drink?

   Sue: a. Yes, please.
   b. Sure.

2. **Bob:** Can I get you a beer?

   Neil: a. Oh, no thanks.
   b. No, I'd rather not, thanks.

3. **Bob:** Do you guys want some food?

   Sue: a. Maybe later.
   b. Not right now, thanks.

◆ IN OTHER WORDS

Read the sentences from the conversation. What do the underlined sentences mean? Choose phrases from Column B that mean the same as the underlined sentences in Column A. Write the correct letter next to each sentence. The first one is done for you.

A

1. **Sue:** I almost didn't make it. _e_

2. **Bob:** Hey, you two! Cut it out. ____

3. **Neil:** No thanks. I don't drink. ____

4. **Bob:** Lost your appetite, Sue? ____

5. **Sue:** He looks familiar. ____

B

a. Stop that!
b. I'm not thirsty.
c. Have a rest.
d. Did you lose your dish, Sue?
e. I almost couldn't come.
f. I don't drink alcohol.
g. Aren't you hungry, Sue?
h. I think I've seen him before.
i. I almost didn't bring any food.
j. He's good-looking.

◆ BETWEEN THE LINES

Bob makes two jokes in the conversation. Read what he says. What do the underlined sentences mean? Circle *a* or *b*.

1. **Bob:** Hey, you two! Cut it out. Where do you think you are?
   Bob means: a. Where do you think you live?
              b. Have you forgotten you're not alone?

2. **Bob:** What?! Lost your appetite, Sue? You know what that means!
   Bob means: a. Sue is not hungry because she just ate.
              b. Sue is not hungry because she is in love.

◆ WORK IT OUT

I We often use interjections to express our feelings. Read the interjections Bob and Sue used. When do we use these words? Match the underlined interjections with the situations.

Interjection

1. **Sue:** Whoops! I've spilled some on your carpet. ____

2. **Bob:** What?! Lost your appetite, Sue? ____

Situation

a. When you drop something

b. When you are surprised

II Do you know these other interjections? Choose a word from the box for each situation. Write the word in the blank.

Phew!	Yuck!	Ouch!

1. You accidentally hit your head as you get into your car. You say "_____!"

2. You thought you failed your driving test. You find out you passed it. You say "_____!"

3. Your two-year-old daughter put chocolate sauce on her hamburger. You say "_____!"

◆ LET'S TALK ABOUT ... DRINKING

In Canada and the United States, people often drink alcoholic beverages at parties or on special occasions. Often you are asked to "bring your own bottle" (BYOB) when you go to a party at someone's house. There are usually nonalcoholic drinks available for those people who don't drink. What about in the culture you come from? Do people drink alcohol? Discuss these questions with your classmates.

1. Is drinking alcohol acceptable in your culture?
2. When do you drink alcohol?
3. Do you "bring your own bottle" to a party, or does the host provide the drinks?

◆ ACT IT OUT

Have a party! Bring to class something to drink and eat. Then choose three people in your class to act as the hosts of the party. The rest of the class are the guests. Role-play the following situation.

➤ **Hosts:** Walk around the room and ask the guests what they would like to eat and drink.

➤ **Guests:** Stand up and talk to the other guests. Tell the host what you want to eat or drink when he or she asks.

Use the sentences below to help you:

Host	**Guest**
What would you like to drink?	Juice/soda/water, please.
Can I get you a drink?	Sure./Yes, please.
Do you want some food?	No, thanks./Not right now, thanks.
Would you like something to eat?	Nothing right now, thanks.

Begin like this:

Host: What would you like to drink?

Guest: Juice, please.

PART TWO

◆ TAKE A GUESS

Look at the title of this episode. What do you think will happen in this part? Discuss your answer with your classmates.

HAVE YOU GOT IT?

Listen to the conversation. Was your guess correct? What happens? Circle the correct answer.

a. Neil asks Sue to marry him.

b. Sue asks Neil to marry her.

CHECK IT OUT

Listen again. Are these sentences correct? Check (✔) *Yes* or *No*.

	Yes	No
1. Sue's mother is at Bob's party.	☐	☐
2. Neil and Sue help Bob clean up.	☐	☐
3. Sue has to go home soon.	☐	☐
4. Neil may go back to India.	☐	☐
5. Neil and Sue say they love each other.	☐	☐

◆ BETWEEN THE LINES

Read the questions. Circle *a* or *b*. Discuss your answers with your classmates.

1. Why does Neil ask Sue to marry him?

   a. He wants to stay in the country.

   b. He loves her.

2. Why doesn't Sue say "yes" right away when Neil asks her to marry him?

   a. She doesn't love Neil.

   b. She knows her parents are arranging a marriage for her.

◆ WHAT DO YOU THINK?

Should Sue marry Neil? Discuss this question with a partner. Make a list of the reasons why she should or should not marry him.

Reasons for Marrying Neil	Reasons Against Marrying Neil
1. *Sue loves Neil*	1. *Sue's arranged marriage*
2. _____	2. _____
3. _____	3. _____
4. _____	4. _____

◆ IN OTHER WORDS

Read the sentences from the conversation. What do the underlined phrases mean? Choose phrases from Column B that mean the same as the underlined phrases in Column A. Write the correct letter next to each sentence. The first one is done for you.

A

1. **Neil:** And knowing that we won't <u>run into</u> your mother! *b*

2. **Sue:** <u>Need a hand</u>, Bob? _____

3. **Sue:** Anyway, it looks like you'll be going back to India pretty soon, doesn't it?

   Neil: Well, <u>not necessarily</u>. _____

4. **Neil:** Something may <u>turn up</u>. _____

B

a. it's not certain
b. meet
c. it's not necessary
d. go around
e. jog after
f. Can I help you?
g. happen
h. Did you hurt your hand?

◆ ACT IT OUT

When Neil asks Sue to marry him, he hesitates. He uses words such as "uh," "well," and "you know" to fill the silence. Read part of his conversation with Sue.

Neil: Well, if we love each other...uh...we could uh...

Sue: What?

Neil: Well, what I'm trying to say is...you know...well, why don't we get married?

Work with a partner. Choose a role and role-play the following situation in front of the class. Then change roles.

◆ **Student A:** You are the mother or father of Student B who has just come home from school. Ask how his or her courses are going.

◆ **Student B:** You are a student and have just failed some important exams for the second time. You have to tell your mother or father. You know she or he will not be happy.

Begin like this:

Student A: How are your courses going, dear?

Student B: Well...I don't know...uh...

◆ LET'S TALK ABOUT . . . HOUSEHOLD ROLES

1 Sue and Neil offered to help Bob clean up after his party. In Canada and the United States, men, women, and children sometimes share household chores such as cleaning, cooking, and making repairs. Look at the chart. In some cultures, only women do these things; in other cultures, it is okay only for men; in others, children may do some of these things. Think about the culture you come from and check (✔) who usually does these things. You may check more than one box for each chore. Then compare your answers with a partner's.

Who:	Women	Men	Children
washes the dishes?			
makes the beds?			
takes out the garbage?			
cleans the home?			
cooks for the family?			
takes care of the children?			
takes care of money matters?			
does household repairs?			

2 Discuss these questions with your classmates.

   a. Are there big differences between the chores that men and women do in different cultures?

   b. Do children do some chores in all cultures?

PART THREE

◆ TAKE A GUESS

Read some words from the conversation. Work with a partner. Try to guess what the conversation will be about.

Neil	sick	doctor	appointment	Sue	call

HAVE YOU GOT IT?

Listen to the conversation. What is the conversation about? Circle the correct answers. There is more than one answer.

a. Neil's proposal

b. Bob's party

c. Neil's illness

CHECK IT OUT

Listen again. Read the statements about Sue and Neil. Check (✔) the information that is correct.

1 Sue

    a. ☐ is at Neil's apartment.

    b. ☐ may have the flu.

    c. ☐ agrees to marry Neil.

2 Neil

    a. ☐ has a fever.

    b. ☐ calls the doctor.

    c. ☐ goes to buy aspirin.

 **DOUBLE-CHECK IT**

Listen again. Fill in the details of Neil's appointment in the doctor's appointment book.

THURSDAY 8	
9:00	
9:15	*Basterfield*
9:30	
9:45	*Haiselden*
10:00	*Chung*
10:15	
10:30	*Morano*
10:45	
11:00	
11:15	
11:30	
11:45	*Valentin*
1:00	*Chadwick*
1:15	

◆ ACT IT OUT

Work with a partner. Choose a role. Role-play the following situation. Then change roles.

Patient: You have a backache. Call the doctor's office and make an appointment with Dr. Cooper for Thursday morning.

Receptionist: You are Dr. Cooper's receptionist. A patient calls to make an appointment. Look at the appointment book in *Double-Check It* and give him or her a suitable time. Write it in the book.

Begin the conversation as in the model. Fill in the blanks as you go.

Receptionist: Good _____ . Dr. Cooper's office.

Patient: I'd like an _____ with Dr. Cooper.

Receptionist: Okay. What's the _____ ?

Patient: I have a _____ .

Receptionist: How about _____ at _____ A.M.?

Patient: That's fine./Do you have anything a little later?

Receptionist: _____

◆ WORK IT OUT

Read the following magazine article. Then answer the questions.

HEALTH &LIFE-STYLE

Do you want to live to be 100? If you do, then follow the example of Mary Higgins. This healthy old lady has just celebrated her one-hundredth birthday. And how has she reached this great age? "I don't eat any sugar, and I go to bed at nine every night," she says. She also walks her dog, Rusty, every day. "Having a dog to walk has kept me fit," she says. How fit? This amazing lady still lives alone (she has never married), does her own shopping and cleaning, and even mows the lawn. The message is: stay active!

1 What does Mary Higgins recommend for a healthy life? Check (✔) the answers. There is more than one answer.

   a. ☐ go to bed early

   b. ☐ don't eat sweet things

   c. ☐ keep a cat

   d. ☐ get married

   e. ☐ stay fit

2 Do you think Mary's lifestyle would give you a long life? Why or why not? Discuss this with your classmates.

◆ LET'S TALK ABOUT... MEDICINE

1 In Canada, the United States, and other Western cultures, doctors often use drugs to treat sickness and disease. In some Eastern cultures, the use of natural remedies, such as herbs, is more common. How is illness treated in your country? Discuss this with your classmates. Complete the chart below.

Culture	Most Common Type of Medicine
North American Indian	*natural remedies*

2 Discuss these questions with your classmates.

   a. In your culture, do you have to pay to see a doctor or is health care paid for by the government?
   b. Is it better one way or the other?

Will She or Won't She?

PART ONE

◆ THINK BACK

What happened in Episode Six? Fill in Sue's journal with words from the box. The first one is done for you.

arrange	kill	marry	love	tell

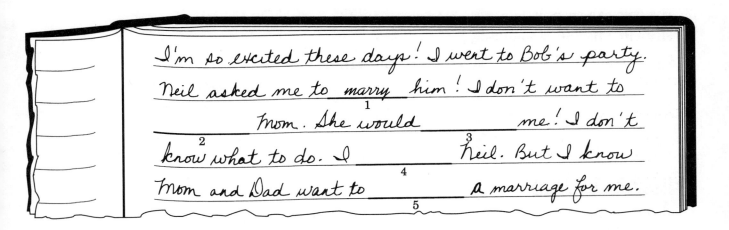

I'm so excited these days! I went to Bob's party. Neil asked me to ____marry____ him! I don't want to
1

____ Mom. She would ____ me! I don't
2   3

know what to do. I ____ Neil. But I know
4

Mom and Dad want to ____ a marriage for me.
5

◆ TAKE A GUESS

Look at the title of this episode. What do you think will happen in the conversation? Discuss this question with your classmates.

📼 HAVE YOU GOT IT?

Listen to the conversation. Complete the sentences. Circle the correct answer.

1. Neil talks to Immigration about how:

   a. a foreign student can get a visa.

   b. a wife can help her husband immigrate.

2. Neil wants to know if Sue:

   a. has decided to marry him.

   b. bought the aspirin.

Listen again. Check (✔) the things that happen in the conversation.

a. ☐ Sue returns from the drugstore with medicine for Neil.

b. ☐ Sue gives Neil a cup of tea.

c. ☐ Sue tells Neil about the aspirin she bought him.

d. ☐ Sue says she wants more time to think about marrying Neil.

e. ☐ At first, Neil doesn't understand why she needs more time.

DOUBLE-CHECK IT

Listen again. What does Immigration tell Neil? Are the sentences correct? Check (✔) *Yes* or *No*. If *No*, correct the sentence.

	Yes	No
1. Neil's wife can sponsor him.	☐	☐
2. His wife can sponsor him if she's a foreign student.	☐	☐
3. His wife fills out an application form.	☐	☐
4. Neil and his wife have an interview at the Immigration office.	☐	☐

◆ BETWEEN THE LINES

Read the questions. Circle your answers. Then discuss your answers with your classmates.

1. Sue needs more time to decide about marrying Neil. How does Neil feel about this?

   a. impatient

   b. jealous

   c. happy

2. Why does Neil feel this way?

   a. His fever is bothering him.

   b. He loves Sue and wants to marry her soon.

   c. He needs to marry so he can immigrate.

◆ ACT IT OUT

Work with a partner. Take turns offering to do things from the list.

◆ Give your partner a ride home. (Your partner has no car.)
◆ Help your partner move. (Your partner is moving to another place.)
◆ Show your partner the best places to shop for groceries. (Your partner is new in town.)

Begin like this:

Student A: Can I give you a ride?

Student B: Sure, that would be great./No, that's Okay.

◆ LET'S TALK ABOUT . . . MULTICULTURALISM

1 Many people immigrate to Canada and the United States. People from different countries live side by side. They often speak different languages, eat different food, and have different lifestyles. Such a society is called "multicultural." Discuss these questions with your classmates.

  a. Is the country you are living in now multicultural?
  b. Is the country you come from multicultural?

2 Look at the chart. Think of other advantages and disadvantages of a multicultural society.

Advantages	Disadvantages
eating different types of food	*fighting between different groups*

PART TWO

◆ TAKE A GUESS

Look at the picture. Then discuss these questions with your classmates.

1. Who are the people?
2. What are they doing?
3. What are they talking about?

📼 HAVE YOU GOT IT?

Listen to the conversation. What are Neil and Dan talking about?
Circle the correct answer.

Neil and Dan are talking about why:

a. Sue and Neil should get married.

b. Neil cannot get another visa.

c. Dan should look for an Indian girlfriend.

🔲 CHECK IT OUT

Listen again. Why does Neil think Sue would be a good wife for him?
Check (✔) the reasons Neil gives.

a. ☐ They're the right ages.

b. ☐ Her parents are from India.

c. ☐ Sue is a good cook.

d. ☐ Sue comes from a good family.

e. ☐ Neil's parents will love Sue.

f. ☐ They both want to have a big family.

◆ IN OTHER WORDS

Read the conversations. What do the underlined words mean? Circle *a* or *b*.

1. **Dan:** That must be the pizza! I hope you're hungry.

   Neil: I'm starving!

   a. I love pizza.

   b. I'm very hungry.

2. **Neil:** Why does she need time? We're a perfect match.

   a. We play well together.

   b. We are a good couple.

3. **Neil:** Well, another thing, her parents are from India, so we have a lot in common!

   a. We have many of the same interests.

   b. We are both ordinary people.

4. **Dan:** That's true. But she's pretty westernized, too. Isn't that a problem?

   a. She acts like she's from a Western culture.

   b. She's a beautiful Western woman.

◆ BODY LANGUAGE

1 Look at the picture in *Take a Guess* on page 66. Neil's index finger is touching his baby finger. What does this mean? Circle the correct answer.

   a. The pizza tastes great.

   b. He is counting reasons.

   c. He is showing Dan his anger.

2 Discuss these questions with your classmates.

   a. Does this gesture mean the same in your culture?

   b. If not, what gesture would you use? Show your classmates.

◆ WHAT DO YOU THINK?

Read these questions. Discuss your answers with your classmates.

1. Are Neil and Sue a perfect match?
2. Does Neil love Sue?
3. Why are Neil's parents coming from India?

◆ WORK IT OUT

Dan ordered pizza over the phone. Put the conversation in order. Number the exchanges from 1 to 6. The first one is done for you.

a. _1_ **Dan:** Hello. I'd like to order two pizzas, please.

 Employee: Yes, what kind would you like?

b. ____ **Dan:** Yes, please. The address is 1360 Cherrywood Road.

 Employee: Cherrywood Road. And the phone number there?

c. ____ **Dan:** Thirty minutes. Great. It's two for one, isn't it?

 Employee: That's right. So it'll be, let's see, $11.95.

d. ____ **Dan:** Great. Thanks a lot. Bye.

e. ____ **Dan:** One twelve-inch green pepper and mushroom pizza and one twelve-inch pepperoni and tomato.

 Employee: Two twelve-inchers. Do you want these delivered?

f. ____ **Dan:** It's 683-2985.

 Employee: 683-2985. Thanks. It'll be about thirty minutes.

◆ ACT IT OUT

Now it's your turn. After studying English so hard, aren't you hungry? Why don't you order a pizza? Take turns ordering different kinds of pizza. Use the model in *Work It Out* and this sample menu.

➤ Pizza Palace Restaurant ◄

555-7373

Delivery hours from 4 P.M. weekdays and from 12 noon weekends

MENU

		9-inch Regular	12-inch Large
Not-So-Basic Cheese Pizza:	A blend of delicious cheeses	$ 5.99	$ 8.99
Grand Slam:	The works: pepperoni, ham, Italian sausage, fresh mushrooms, green peppers, onions, and olives	$ 8.99	$10.99
Hawaiian:	Ham and pineapple..	$ 6.99	$ 8.99
Vegetarian:	Mushrooms and green peppers...................................	$ 5.99	$ 7.99
Special:	Pepperoni and tomatoes	$ 5.99	$ 7.99
Extra Toppings:	(Choice of 14)	$ .99	$ 1.29
Soft Drinks:	Cola, diet cola, ginger ale, root beer	$ 1.50	

TWO FOR ONE!!   *Buy one 12-inch pizza and get a second one FREE!!*

Toppings: Fresh mushrooms, pepperoni, ham, pineapple, Italian sausage, meatballs, green peppers, onions, anchovies, fresh tomatoes, black olives, salami, shrimp, extra cheese

---

◆ WHAT ABOUT YOU?

Read the questions. Discuss your answers with a partner.

1. Do you like take-out food?
2. What kind of food do you like to take out?

◆ LET'S TALK ABOUT . . . FALLING IN LOVE

In Canada and the United States, people usually fall in love first, and then they get married. Sometimes a couple lives together before getting married. In other cultures, love comes after many years of marriage, and living together before marriage is unacceptable. Discuss these questions with your classmates.

1. Do people fall in love before or after they get married?
2. Is living together before marriage acceptable?

PART THREE

📼 HAVE YOU GOT IT?

Listen to the conversation. What is Sue worried about? Complete the sentence below. Circle the correct answer.

Sue is worried that Neil wants to:

a. marry her so he can immigrate.

b. return to India and that she won't see him again.

c. talk to her parents about marrying her.

📼 CHECK IT OUT

Listen again. Sue is suspicious about why Neil wants to marry her. Check (✔) the reasons she gives.

1. ☐ Neil asked Sue how to stay in the country.
2. ☐ At the art gallery, Neil asked Sue to pay.
3. ☐ Neil said they could have a marriage of convenience.
4. ☐ Sue thinks the people in the library were talking about Neil.
5. ☐ Neil was talking on the phone to Immigration.

◆ BETWEEN THE LINES

How does Bob feel about the things Sue says? Circle the correct answers.

1. How does Bob feel when Sue tells him about Neil's proposal?

   a. happy

   b. nervous

   c. angry

2. How does Bob feel when Sue says that Neil just wants to marry her to immigrate?

   a. surprised

   b. insulted

   c. scared

3. How does Bob feel after Sue explains her reasons for believing this?

   a. sad

   b. worried

   c. excited

◆ WHAT DO YOU THINK?

Neil wants to marry Sue. Read these questions. Discuss your answers with your classmates.

1. Should Sue be suspicious about Neil's reasons for marrying her?
2. What do you think Neil will say when Sue talks to him?

◆ IN OTHER WORDS

Read the sentences from the conversation. What do the underlined words mean? Choose phrases from Column B that mean the same as the underlined phrases in Column A. Write the correct letter next to each sentence. The first one is done for you.

A

1. But something's really underlined bugging me. *e*

2. The smoke in this place. It's underlined unbelievable. ____

3. Well, sure, because he doesn't know underlined the system here. ____

4. And now he wants to marry you? This underlined doesn't look good. ____

5. You have to talk to Neil about it. underlined Right away. ____

B

a. immediately
b. how things are done
c. is a bad situation
d. the machine
e. bothering
f. hard to believe
g. not realistic
h. That's the correct way.
i. isn't beautiful

◆ LET'S TALK ABOUT...SMOKING

Many people know the dangers of smoking. In public places in Canada and the United States, there is often a no-smoking area where people are not allowed to smoke. Sometimes smoking isn't allowed in a whole building. Examples of places that have no-smoking areas are restaurants, theaters, and hospitals. Work with a partner. Discuss your answers to these questions.

1. Do you smoke?
2. Does smoke bother you?
3. Do you like places that have no-smoking areas?
4. If another person is smoking and you don't like it, do you say something?
5. Do you let people smoke in your home?
6. Is smoking common in the country you are from? If yes, do both men and women smoke?
7. Are no-smoking areas common in the country you are from?

Hard Decisions

EPISODE EIGHT

PART ONE

◆ THINK BACK

What happened in Episode Seven? Complete these sentences.

1. Neil talks to an immigration officer about _____ .
2. Neil talks to _____ about falling in love with Sue.
3. Sue talks to _____ about her suspicions about Neil.

◆ TAKE A GUESS

Read these three sentences from the conversation. Then answer the questions below. Discuss your answers with your classmates.

◆ "Mother! Father! Over here!"

◆ "Come here, my son!"

◆ "How was your flight?"

1. Who is talking?
2. Where does this conversation take place?

HAVE YOU GOT IT?

Form two groups, Group A and Group B. Follow these steps.

Group A

1. Leave the room. (Group B listens to the conversation.)
2. Find a partner from Group B.
3. To find out what happened in the conversation, ask your partner questions. You may ask the questions in *Take a Guess* or think of others.

Group B

1. Listen to the conversation. (Group A leaves the room.)
2. Find a partner from Group A.
3. Answer your partner's questions about the conversation. Remember that he or she has not heard the conversation yet and does not know what happened.

◆ 72 ◆

Listen again. What do Neil and his parents talk about? Put the pictures in the correct order. Number them from 1 to 3.

a. _____   b. _____   c. _____

 DOUBLE-CHECK IT

Listen again. Look at the flight arrival and departure boards. Then do the following:

1. Circle the flight numbers you hear.
2. Write the gate number you hear.

ARRIVALS			
FLIGHT	**TIME**	**GATE**	**ORIGIN**
Trans-Ocean 274	16:15	Customs	London
Trans-Ocean 264	18:05	Customs	London

DEPARTURES			
FLIGHT	**TIME**	**GATE**	**DESTINATION**
Maple Leaf Air 447	14:50	_____	Vancouver
Maple Leaf Air 457	15:20	1	Vancouver

◆ IN OTHER WORDS

Read these sentences from the conversation. What do they mean?
Circle *a* or *b*.

1. **Mrs. Chandra:** You need somebody to look after you.

   a. You need somebody to look behind you.

   b. You need somebody to take care of you.

2. **Neil:** I'm not the best cook in the world.

   a. I don't know how to cook.

   b. I'm not a very good cook.

3. **Mr. Chandra:** I think she's ready for grandchildren.

   a. I think she would like to have grandchildren.

   b. I think she has to get her grandchildren ready.

◆ WHAT DO YOU THINK?

Work with a partner. Discuss these questions.

1. Will Neil marry the young lady his mother wrote him about?
2. Why or why not?

◆ LET'S TALK ABOUT...FINES

In Canada and the United States, people pay a fine (money) for doing illegal things. Some examples of things that are against the law are speeding, parking illegally, jaywalking, and littering. What about in the country you come from? Do people pay fines for these things? Check (✔) those items for which people pay fines. Discuss your answers with your classmates.

Do people in your country pay fines for:

a. ☐ speeding?

b. ☐ parking illegally?

c. ☐ jaywalking?

d. ☐ littering?

e. ☐ smoking in elevators?

f. ☐ not cutting the lawn?

g. ☐ other _____

PART TWO

◆ TAKE A GUESS

Sue and Neil run into each other at a drugstore. What do you think
they will talk about? Check (✔) the topics. Discuss your answers with
your classmates.

a. ☐ medicine

b. ☐ their future

c. ☐ food

d. ☐ prices

HAVE YOU GOT IT?

Listen to the conversation. Then fill in Sue's journal with words from
the box.

no	Neil	parents	marry	Dan
date	yes	park	friends	restaurant

_This afternoon I ran into _____ at the drugstore._
                                    1
_We went to a _____ to talk. He told me that his_
                      2
_____ want him to marry an Indian girl who_
3
lives here, but he doesn't want to. I realize now
_that Neil wants to _____ me because he really_
                          4
loves me. He asked me to marry him, and I said
_____ . This is the happiest day of my life !_
     5

CHECK IT OUT

Listen again. Are these sentences correct? Check (✔) *Yes* or *No*. If *No*, correct the sentence.

	Yes	No
1. Sue went to the drugstore because she has strep throat.	☐	☐
2. Neil has a bad headache.	☐	☐
3. Dr. Cooper gave Neil a prescription for antibiotics.	☐	☐
4. Neil has had a prescription filled at that drugstore before.	☐	☐

DOUBLE-CHECK IT

Listen again. Answer the questions. Circle the correct answer.

1. What is Neil's full name?

   a. Neil Chamdra

   b. Neil Chandra

   c. Neil Chandre

2. What is Neil's address?

   a. 1316 Cherrywood Road, #70

   b. 3060 Cherrywood Road, #17

   c. 1360 Cherrywood Road, #17

3. What is Neil's phone number?

   a. 683-2585

   b. 683-2985

   c. 683-3985

4. How long does Neil have to wait for his medicine?

   a. 5 minutes

   b. 15 minutes

   c. 50 minutes

◆ BETWEEN THE LINES

Complete the sentences. Circle *a*, *b*, or *c*. Then discuss your answers in small groups.

1. When Sue says she is relieved, Neil feels:

   a. shocked.

   b. jealous.

   c. scared.

2. Neil feels this way because he:

   a. thought Sue would not marry him.

   b. didn't know Sue suspected him.

   c. thought that Sue was in love with Bob.

◆ ACT IT OUT

Work with a partner. Choose a role and role-play the following situation. Then change roles.

➤ **Pharmacist:** Ask your customer questions so you can fill out the customer form below.

➤ **Customer:** Answer the pharmacist's questions.

Begin like this:

Pharmacist: What's your full name?

Customer: _____ .

```
        🥣 DRUGS AND MORE
        Customer Information Form
```

Name _____

Address _____

_____

Birthdate _____
           mo.   day   yr.

Sex   M   F

Phone Number _____

PART THREE ‿‿‿‿‿‿‿‿‿‿‿‿‿‿‿‿‿‿‿

◆ TAKE A GUESS

Use the clues to solve the riddle. Write the answers to the clues in the blanks. The first one is done for you.

Clues

1. The girl Neil is in love with
2. Another word for *speak*
3. Mothers and fathers are called this
4. The opposite of *unimportant*

_____*Sushila*_____ will _____ to her _____
       1   2   3

about something very _____ .
                      4

Now can you guess what will happen in Part Three? Discuss it with your classmates.

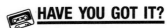 **HAVE YOU GOT IT?**

Listen to the conversation. Answer the question. Circle the correct answer.

What does Sushila tell her parents?

a. She decided to marry Neil.

b. She decided to move to India.

c. She will never see Neil again.

CHECK IT OUT

Listen again. Complete the sentences with words from the box.

unhappy	agree	safety	forbid
disagree	cooking	tired	want

1. Sushila and her mother talk about _____ in the kitchen.

2. Sushila's parents _____ with her decision.

3. Sushila's parents _____ Sushila to see Neil again.

4. Sushila feels very _____ .

DOUBLE-CHECK IT

Listen again. Complete the statements. Circle the correct answer.

1. Mrs. Chopra is worried about the nail polish because it could:

   a. stain the burners.

   b. start a fire.

2. Sushila thinks her mother is:

   a. wrong.

   b. right.

WHAT DO YOU THINK?

Work with a partner. Discuss the questions. Give reasons for your opinions.

1. Will Sushila's parents change their minds?
2. What do you think will happen next?

◆ WORK IT OUT

Work with a partner. Discuss the meaning of the safety symbols. Then draw and discuss with your teacher the meaning of other symbols that you know.

Safety Symbols

Other Symbols You Know

◆ LET'S TALK ABOUT . . . SAFETY

In Canada and the United States, people and the government are careful about safety in the home and in public places. In other words, they are "safety conscious." Many symbols are used to warn people about danger. Discuss these questions in small groups.

1. Are safety symbols used in the culture you come from?
2. Which safety symbols are common in the culture you come from?
3. In what other ways are people warned about danger?

Heartbreak

PART ONE

◆ THINK BACK

What happened in Episode Eight? Read these sentences from Episode Eight. Who said them? Write *Mr. Chopra*, *Neil*, *Sue*, or *Mrs. Chandra*.

1. "Mother! Father! Over here!"   _____

2. "Have you thought about the young lady I wrote you about?"   _____

3. "Of course I'll marry you!"   _____

4. "Mom, Dad, I've made a decision."   _____

5. "We forbid you to see that young man ever again!"   _____

◆ TAKE A GUESS

Sue goes to Bob's apartment. What do you think she wants to talk about? Check (✔) the topics. Discuss your answers with your classmates.

a. ☐ homework

b. ☐ her parents

c. ☐ Neil

d. ☐ Bob's problems

e. ☐ the weather

📼 HAVE YOU GOT IT?

Listen to the conversation. Were your answers to *Take a Guess* correct? If not, discuss the corrections.

🔲 CHECK IT OUT

Listen again. Complete the sentences. Circle the correct answer.

1. Sue was late because:

    a. she was feeling terrible.

    b. she missed her bus.

    c. she had to make a phone call.

2. Sue tells Bob:

    a. her parents have forbidden her to see Neil again.

    b. about her decision.

    c. she will run away with Neil.

3. Bob suggests Sue:

    a. call Neil from his house.

    b. talk to her parents.

    c. stop seeing Neil.

🔲 DOUBLE-CHECK IT

Listen again. Read these sentences. Write *T* if the sentence is true. Write *F* if the sentence is false. Correct the false sentences.

1. _____ Sue feels happy when she gets to Bob's apartment.

2. _____ Bob wants Sue and Neil to talk about their future.

3. _____ Sue is scared her parents will see Neil and her together.

4. _____ Sue will ask Neil to come to Bob's apartment.

5. _____ Bob will stay with Sue and Neil while they talk.

◆ WHAT ABOUT YOU?

Work with a partner. Read the question. Circle *a* or *b* or write your own answer.

What would you do if you were Sue?

a. Elope with Neil.

b. Not see Neil again.

c. Other _____

◆ LET'S TALK ABOUT . . . PUNCTUALITY

1 Sue apologized to Bob for being late. In Canada and the United States, being on time (being punctual) is usually very important. In what situations is punctuality important in the culture you come from? Read the questions and check (✔) *Yes* or *No*.

Is it okay to arrive:

	Yes	No
a. 15 minutes late for a business appointment?	☐	☐
b. 30 minutes late for a dinner party?	☐	☐
c. 20 minutes late for a visit to a friend's house?	☐	☐
d. 15 minutes late for a dental appointment?	☐	☐

2 Discuss your answers with your classmates. Is punctuality more important in some cultures than it is in others?

◆ ACT IT OUT

Work with a partner. Choose a role and role-play the following situation. Then change roles.

Student A: You have agreed to meet Student B at the library at 9:00 A.M. You get there on time and have to wait 30 minutes for Student B.

Student B: You have agreed to meet Student A at the library at 9:00 A.M. You are 30 minutes late because your car wouldn't start. Explain to Student A what happened and apologize for being late.

Begin like this:

Student A: What happened to you?

Student B: I'm really sorry . . .

PART TWO

◆ TAKE A GUESS

Sue and Neil meet at Bob's apartment. What will they decide to do about their future? Circle your answer. Then discuss your answer with your classmates.

a. elope

b. separate

c. talk to their parents

HAVE YOU GOT IT?

Listen to the conversation. What do Sue and Neil decide to do? Discuss your answer with your classmates.

CHECK IT OUT

Listen again. Are these sentences correct? Check (✔) *Yes* or *No*. If *No*, correct the sentence.

	Yes	No
1. Sue and Neil talk about their problem.	☐	☐
2. Sue leaves Bob's apartment.	☐	☐
3. Neil breaks out crying.	☐	☐

DOUBLE-CHECK IT

Listen again. Neil makes some suggestions. Check (✔) whether Sue agrees or disagrees. The first one is done for you.

	Sue Agrees	Sue Disagrees
1. Neil suggests his parents talk to Sue's parents.	☐	✔
2. Neil doesn't think eloping is possible.	☐	☐
3. Neil thinks it might help if he talks to Sue's parents.	☐	☐
4. Neil suggests Sue talk to her parents again.	☐	☐
5. Neil thinks they should not see each other again.	☐	☐

◆ WHAT DO YOU THINK?

Work with a partner. Discuss these questions. Give reasons for your opinions.

1. Should Sue and Neil break up?
2. Why or why not?

◆ LET'S TALK ABOUT . . . CRYING

1   When Neil leaves, Sue breaks out crying. In Canada and the United
    States, people do not usually cry in public. In private, both men and
    women may cry. What about in the culture you come from? Read
    the questions and check (✔) *Yes* or *No*.

Is it okay for a woman:

	Yes	No
a. to cry in public?	☐	☐
b. to cry in private?	☐	☐

Is it okay for a man:

	Yes	No
a. to cry in public?	☐	☐
b. to cry in private?	☐	☐

2   Discuss your answers with your classmates. What are the differences
    and similarities between cultures?

PART THREE

◆ TAKE A GUESS

Look at the two pictures. They are almost the same. Can you find the
six differences? Work with a partner. Discuss the differences between
the two pictures. Then answer the questions that follow.

1. What are Sue and her mother doing?
2. Why?

📼 HAVE YOU GOT IT?

Listen to the conversation. Which of the two pictures from *Take A Guess* shows best what happens? Discuss your answer with your classmates.

📼 CHECK IT OUT

Listen again. Complete the summary. Choose the correct words and write them in the blanks. The first one is done for you.

Sushila and her mother ___*drop off*___ the _____
                               1. drop off/throw out   2. recyclable/smelly

garbage. Then they go to the East Indian Boutique to buy something

to wear at next _____ 's party. They buy a beautiful
                       3. Sunday/Saturday

_____ that suits Sue very well. At this party, Sue will
4. dress/sari

meet her future _____ .
                        5. husband/classmate

📼 DOUBLE-CHECK IT

Listen again. Fill in the amount, the tax, and the total on Mrs. Chopra's VISTA bill.

```
 357 338 6673 3889
 ─── DO NOT WRITE ABOVE THIS LINE ───
```

| | | AUTHORIZATION NO. |
| | | *13174* |

PIA CHOPRA   EXPIRATION ☑ DATE   BILL NO.
CHECKED

DATE *10-3-94*   CLERK *DP*

EAST INDIAN BOUTIQUE
372 RIVER SIDE STREET   10 546 120

			AMOUNT
			TAX
			TIPS
			TOTAL

CUSTOMER COPY

SALES DRAFT

CARDHOLDER'S SIGNATURE

x *Pia Chopra*

PLEASE RETAIN
THIS COPY FOR
YOUR RECORDS

VISTA

Cardholder will pay to issuer of the
charge card presented herewith the amount
stated hereon in accordance with issuer's
agreement with the cardholder.

◆ ACT IT OUT

Work with a partner. Choose a role and role-play the following situation using the sentences that follow. Then change roles.

◆ **Customer:** You are shopping for a sweater for yourself.

◆ **Clerk:** Help your customer find what he or she is looking for.

Use the sentences below to help you:

Clerk	Customer
Can I help you?	Can I try it/them on?
What size do you wear?	It fits/doesn't fit me.
I'll get you a smaller/bigger size.	It's too small/big/tight/loose.
That really suits/doesn't suit you.	It's too long/short.

Begin like this:

Clerk: Good morning. Can I help you?

Customer: Yes, please. I'm looking for a sweater.

◆ BODY LANGUAGE

1 Look at the picture in *Take a Guess* on page 84. What does the salesclerk's hand gesture mean? Circle *a*, *b*, or *c*.

   a. You look great!

   b. There's a hole in the sari.

   c. The sari is on sale.

2 Discuss these questions with your classmates.

   a. Does this gesture mean the same in your culture?
   b. If not, what gesture would you use? Show your classmates.

◆ LET'S TALK ABOUT . . . RECYCLING

In Canada and the United States, people recycle some of their garbage, such as bottles, cans, paper, and plastics. *Recycling* garbage means that this garbage is used to make other products. Discuss the following questions with your classmates.

1. Is garbage recycled in the country you come from?
2. Do you think it's a good idea to recycle garbage? Why or why not?

Guess What!

PART ONE

◆ THINK BACK

What happened in Episode Nine? Read the entry in Sushila's journal and correct the mistakes. The first one is done for you.

> I met Bob today. He suggested that ~~Dan~~ ^{Neil} and I elope. What an idea! Anyway, Mom came over to Bob's apartment, and we talked. Neil and I decided we should stay together. I feel so excited. Later Dad took me shopping for a new sweater. They're having a party for me to meet my future boss.

◆ TAKE A GUESS

Sushila and her mother are getting ready for the party where Sushila will meet her future husband. What do you think they are talking about? Check your answers.

a. ☐ food   c. ☐ money

b. ☐ clothes   d. ☐ marriage

📼 HAVE YOU GOT IT?

1 Listen to the conversation. Were your answers to *Take a Guess* correct? If not, discuss the corrections.

2 Put the sentences in the correct order. Number them from 1 to 3.

a. _____ Sushila goes upstairs.

b. _____ Neil calls.

c. _____ Mrs. Chopra talks about the food.

📼 CHECK IT OUT

Listen again. Read the sentences. Write *T* if the sentence is correct. Write *F* if the sentence is false. Correct the false sentences.

1. _____ The food Mrs. Chopra prepared is North American.

2. _____ Mrs. Chopra made two types of curry.

3. _____ Sushila tries her mother's cookies.

4. _____ Sushila isn't hungry.

5. _____ Mrs. Chopra knows the parents of Sushila's future husband.

📼 DOUBLE-CHECK IT

Listen again. Answer the questions. Circle *a*, *b*, or *c*.

1. Why does Neil call Sue?

   a. to tell her he loves her

   b. to ask her to meet him

   c. to tell her something important

2. What does Sue tell Neil?

   a. She is busy.

   b. She can't talk to him.

   c. He should not call her again.

◆ BETWEEN THE LINES

How do the people feel? Circle your answers. Discuss your answers with your classmates.

1. Mrs. Chopra feels happy/sad about the party.

2. Sue feels unhappy/nervous about the party.

3. Sue feels upset/pleased about Neil's phone call.

4. Neil sounds angry/excited on the phone.

◆ WHAT DO YOU THINK?

Work with a partner. Discuss these questions.

1. What does Neil want to tell Sue?
2. Should Sue listen to Neil?

◆ WORK IT OUT

Read the restaurant review. Then answer the questions.

THE BOMBAY PALACE

For a (wonderful) spicy treat, try this small East Indian restaurant on George Street. Start with one of the delicious appetizers, which include some tasty vegetable p a k o r a s (deep-fried vegetables). For a main dish, sample one of the numerous curries, or for a change why not try a biryani (rice dish). Then finish off with one of the delectable desserts. A tasty three-course meal will cost about $30 for two people, including drinks and tip.

1 Which words in the review have the following meanings? Write the word in the blank.

a. the first course of a meal   _____

b. the biggest course   _____

c. the last course   _____

2 Does the review say the restaurant is good? Circle all the words that are positive. The first one is done for you.

◆ LET'S TALK ABOUT ... FOOD

In Canada and the United States, some typical foods are steak, fried chicken, ribs, and french fries. "Fast-food" restaurants are popular. They provide a meal in a few minutes. Some examples of fast foods are hot dogs, burgers, and pizza. Work with a partner. Discuss the following questions.

1. What are some typical foods in the country you come from?
2. Do you have fast foods in the country you come from? If so, what are some typical fast foods?
3. What is your favorite dish?

PART TWO

◆ TAKE A GUESS

The Chopras' doorbell rings. Who is at the door? Check your answer.

a. ☐ Sushila's future parents-in-law

b. ☐ the Chopras' neighbors

c. ☐ old friends of the Chopras'

🎞 HAVE YOU GOT IT?

Listen to the conversation. Read the two summaries below. Which summary describes the conversation? Check (✔) A or B.

☐ A. Mr. and Mrs. Chopra welcome their guests, Amit and Monisha and their son. They talk about life in India.

☐ B. Mr. Chopra welcomes the guests, Amit and Monisha. They talk about their families.

🎞 CHECK IT OUT

Listen again. Answer the questions. Check (✔) *Mr. Chopra*, *Sushila*, or *Amit's son*.

	Mr. Chopra	Sushila	Amit's son
1. Who has been in North America a long time?	☐	☐	☐
2. Who is upstairs?	☐	☐	☐
3. Who is parking the car?	☐	☐	☐
4. Who is smart?	☐	☐	☐
5. Who is busy studying?	☐	☐	☐

🎞 DOUBLE-CHECK IT

Listen again. Read the questions. Circle the correct answers. The first one is done for you.

1. How many years has Mr. Chopra been in North America?	24	(25)	35
2. How many more years will Sushila study?	1	2	3
3. How many sons does Amit have?	1	2	3
4. How many children does Amit have in India?	2	3	4
5. How many children does Amit's brother Anil have?	2	3	4

◆ WORK IT OUT

Look at Amit's family tree. Then answer the questions. Write your answers in the blanks. The first one is done for you.

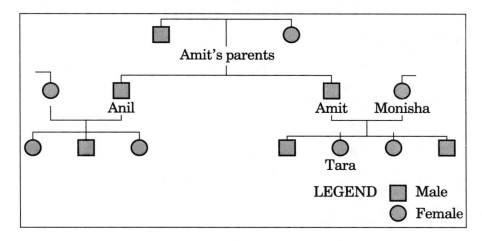

1. How many grandchildren do Amit's parents have? _____7_____

2. Who is Tara's uncle? _____

3. How many cousins does Tara have? _____

4. Who is Anil's sister-in-law? _____

5. How many nieces and nephews does Amit have? _____

6. Who is the aunt of Anil's children? _____

7. How many brothers does Tara have? _____

◆ ACT IT OUT

Work with a partner. Ask each other about your families. Draw your partner's family tree on a separate piece of paper.

Begin like this:

Student A: Do you come from a large family?

Student B: Yes, I have three brothers and a sister./No, I only have one sister.

◆ LET'S TALK ABOUT ... FAMILIES

In Canada and the United States, the "nuclear" family (parents and children living together) is the common family unit. Most families have two or three children. Single-parent families are also common. In these families, children live with one parent. This is usually the result of divorce. In some cultures, people live in "extended" families—that is parents, grandparents, children, aunts, uncles, and cousins all living together. What about in the culture you come from? Discuss the following questions with a partner.

1. Do most people live in nuclear or in extended families?
2. How many children do people usually have?
3. Are single-parent families common?

PART THREE

◆ TAKE A GUESS

Sue will meet the young man her parents want her to marry. What do you think Sue's reaction will be? Check (✔) your answer. Discuss your answer with your classmates.

1. ☐ She will like the young man.
2. ☐ She won't like the young man.
3. ☐ She will run away before the young man arrives.

🎞 HAVE YOU GOT IT?

Listen to the conversation. Complete the sentence. Choose the correct words and write them in the blanks.

When _____ answers the door,
     1. Mrs. Chopra/Mrs. Chandra/Sushila

she sees _____ and then realizes he is her
     2. a stranger/Neil/Bob

_____ .
3. future husband/friend/classmate

🎞 CHECK IT OUT

Listen again. Complete the sentences. Circle the correct answers.

1. At first, Sue thought Neil:

    a. wanted to talk to her about their love.

    b. was her future husband.

    c. had the wrong address.

2. Neil goes to Sue's house because:

    a. someone gives him wrong directions.

    b. he wants to elope with Sue.

    c. his parents want him to meet a young woman.

🎞 DOUBLE-CHECK IT

Listen again. Are these sentences correct? Check (✔) *Yes* or *No*. If *No*, correct the sentence.

	Yes	No
1. Mr. Chopra asks Sue to answer the door.	☐	☐
2. Sue tries to tell Neil something.	☐	☐
3. Sue and Neil met about six months ago.	☐	☐
4. Mrs. Chopra is happy that Sue and Neil will now be together.	☐	☐
5. Mrs. Chandra and Mrs. Chopra think that Sue and Neil's reunion is destiny.	☐	☐

◆ LET'S TALK ABOUT ... COINCIDENCES AND DESTINY

In Canada and the United States, some people believe that things in a person's life happen by accident. These people believe in "coincidences." Others think that certain things will happen to people, no matter what they do. These people believe in "destiny." What about in the culture you come from? Work with a partner and discuss the following questions.

1. Do most people in the culture you come from believe in coincidences or destiny?
2. What do you believe in, coincidences or destiny?

◆ WORK IT OUT

Form two teams, Team A and Team B. Follow these steps and keep score in the chart below. The team with the highest number of points wins!

Team A

1. A student on your team tells Team B a story about a coincidence. The story may be real or imaginary.
2. Change roles. A student on Team B tells your team a story. Guess if it is real or imaginary. If you guess right, your team wins a point.

Team B

1. A student on Team A tells your team a story about a coincidence. Guess if it is real or imaginary. If you guess right, your team wins a point.
2. Change roles. A student on your team tells Team A a story. The story may be real or imaginary.

Team A	Team B

Here is an example of a story about a coincidence:

I went on vacation to Vancouver last summer, and I ran into my next-door neighbor.

Tapescript

◆ EPISODE ONE

PART ONE

Mrs. Chopra: Tsk, tsk, tsk. That's terrible!

Mr. Chopra: What is it, dear?

Mrs. Chopra: I'm reading an article on marriages of convenience. They're up 50 percent!

Mr. Chopra: Up 50 percent?! That's a lot.

Sue: What are marriages of convenience, anyway?

Mrs. Chopra: That's when a person gets married in order to stay in another country.

Mr. Chopra: That's right. People marry just to live in another country!

Sue: Well, I think that's wrong. Anyway, who would want a marriage of convenience?

Mr. Chopra: Maybe students, or people in trouble in their own country...

Mrs. Chopra: You know, maybe political or religious trouble...

Sue: Or daughters with parents that don't let them do anything.

Mrs. Chopra: Sushila, really!

Sue: Well, I have to go.

Mr. Chopra: Where are you going?

Sue: I'm going to the hockey game.

Mr. Chopra: With Bob?

Sue: Yes, Dad.

Mr. Chopra: OK, Sushila, but be home by 11 o'clock...

Sue: Eleven?! I'm not a child anymore.

Mr. Chopra: We know that, dear, but it's not right for a young lady to be out too late.

Sue: But Dad...

Mrs. Chopra: Please, dear. Do as your father says. And don't forget your jacket.

Sue: Wow! How old do you think I am?! See you later.

Mr. Chopra: Bye, dear.

Mrs. Chopra: Have a nice time! Children these days!

PART TWO

Sue: Bob!

Bob: Sue. Sorry I'm late. Has the game started?

Sue: No, no. We've still got five minutes.

Bob: Let's look at the tickets. Where are we sitting?

Sue: Um...section M, row fourteen, seats six and seven.

Bob: Row fourteen. Those are good seats.

Sue: Mm. We'll get a great view of the ice from there.

Bob: Yeah. Hey! There's a guy from my math class. Hey, Neil!

Neil: Oh hi, Bob.

Bob: Sue, this is Neil.

Sue: Hi.

Bob: He's in my math class. Neil, this is Sue. Her real name's Sushila, but everyone calls her Sue.

Neil: Hi. Nice to meet you, Sue.

Sue: Nice to meet you, too. Do you often come to the hockey games?

Neil: No. In fact, this is my first time.

Sue: Oh, really?

Neil: Yes. I thought I should come to a game. Everyone seems to be crazy about hockey.

Sue: Well, I'm a fan, too. But not like Bob!

Neil: I know what you mean. That's all he talks about!

Bob: Well, it's about time you came to a game. How long have you been here now?

Neil: Mm...about eighteen months.

Bob: Neil's from India, Sue. Like your folks.

Neil: Where are you from in India?

Sue: Well, my parents are from Delhi. But I was born here.

Bob: We'd better get to our seats. The game's going to start.

Sue: OK, OK.

Bob: How about meeting us after the game, Neil? We're going to a restaurant.

Neil: Sure. That sounds great.

Bob: Let's meet back here then after the game.

Neil: OK.

Sue and Bob: Bye. See you later.

PART THREE

Sue: Great game! The best this season!

Bob: I agree. You chose a good night to watch your first hockey game, Neil.

Neil: Yeah, it was very exciting!

Sue: It's always exciting to see your team win.

Bob: Yeah! And what a score! Five to one!

Sue: So...will you come to the next hockey game, Neil?

Neil: I don't know. I'm very busy studying.

Bob: Neil's a bookworm, Sue.

Neil: Yeah...well...you know, I came here to go to the university.

Sue: What are you studying?

Neil: Engineering. What about you?

Sue: I'm taking chemistry. When will you finish your studies?

Neil: In six months, and then, unfortunately, I'll have to go back to India.

Sue: How come?

Neil: I'm here on a student visa, and I'll have to leave as soon as I finish.

Sue: Oh, I see. You must miss your folks.

Neil: You bet! And they miss me a lot, too.

Sue: I'm sure. Talking about parents...we should get going. I promised my parents I'd be home by eleven, and it's already midnight.

Bob: OK. Let's go.

Sue: How much is the bill?

Bob: Don't worry about it. It's my turn to pay. You paid last time.

Sue: OK.

Neil: How much do I owe you?

Bob: Oh, that's OK. You can get it next time.

Neil: I guess this means we'll get together again.

Sue: Sure. Bob and I are going to the movies next Saturday. Would you like to join us?

Neil: Yeah, I'd like that. What are you going to see?

Bob: Oh, we don't know yet. Here. I'll give you my phone number.

Neil: OK.

Bob: Give me a call sometime this week.

Neil: Sure.

◆ **_EPISODE TWO_**

PART ONE

Pat: Sue! Over here!

Sue: Hi, Pat.

Pat: Hi. How are you?

Sue: Terrible! I have three assignments for one class next week!

Pat: That means Miss Chopra won't be going out this weekend?

Sue: Not a chance! I'll do them. I want to see Neil again.

Pat: Really?

Sue: Yeah. He seems very nice, and he's just my type.

Pat: Ah-ha! And what type is that?

Sue: Well, he's quite tall. And he has a moustache.

Pat: Ugh! You like hairy faces?

Sue: Not beards! Just moustaches. And...

Pat: And?

Sue: And he's got beautiful brown eyes. I think he's really handsome.

Pat: Oh, you do?

Sue: Yeah, especially with that curly black hair.

Pat: Well, I hear he's a really nice guy, Sue. But I think he's very busy studying. He wouldn't have time for you.

Sue: Oh, you don't think so?

Pat: Bob says he's very serious about his degree and getting the best grades he can.

Sue: Well, maybe we can study together.

Pat: Then he'll never get his degree. But seriously, I thought your parents were arranging a marriage for you.

Sue: Yeah, that's right. They're going to find me a husband.

Pat: Do you know who he is?

Sue: No, Pat, not yet.

Pat: Well, then, don't worry. Enjoy yourself!

Sue: Yeah, I guess so. So are you going out with anyone?

Pat: No, not right now. But I might be very soon!

PART TWO

Mrs. Chopra: Hello.

Neil: Hello. Is Sue there, please?

Mrs. Chopra: No, she isn't.

Neil: Oh, um, well, can I leave a message?

Mrs. Chopra: Go ahead.

Neil: Please tell her Neil called.

Mrs. Chopra: Neil?

Neil: Yes, Neil. Please tell her that Bob...

Mrs. Chopra: Bob?

Neil: Yes. Bob can't go to the movies.

Mrs. Chopra: Can't go to the movies.

Neil: He's not feeling well.

Mrs. Chopra: He's sick. Is that all?

Neil: Um, no. Tell Sue I'm still going.

Mrs. Chopra: *You're* going to the movies.

Neil: Yes.

Mrs. Chopra: Anything else?

Neil: Well, could you ask her to call me?

Mrs. Chopra: Call you?

Neil: Yes. My number is 683-2985.

Mrs. Chopra: 683-2985. Is that all?

Neil: Yes. Thank you very much.

Mrs. Chopra: You're welcome.

Neil: Good-bye.

Mrs. Chopra: Good-bye.

PART THREE

Mrs. Chopra: Sushila, is that you?

Sue: Yes, Mom.

Mrs. Chopra: Come here, please.

Sue: Yes, Mom?

Mrs. Chopra: Here. It's a message from Neil.

Sue: Oh. Thanks.

Mrs. Chopra: Sushila, I want to know who this Neil is. Who is he?

Sue: He's just a friend of Bob's.

Mrs. Chopra: Sushila, I've told you so many, many times before.

Sue: But Mom!

Mrs. Chopra: You are not to go out with boys your father and I don't know.

Sue: But Mom, I just met him. I don't even know him.

Mrs. Chopra: Well, then why are you going to a movie with him?

Sue: So I can get to know him!

Mrs. Chopra: Look. It's all right to go out with Bob. We know him. But this Neil...

Sue: Mom, please! Let me choose my own friends.

Mrs. Chopra: Girlfriends only! Not boys!

Sue: But Mom, I'm twenty-one years old. This is ridiculous.

Mrs. Chopra: Ridiculous!? Why is it so ridiculous?

Sue: Because other people my age choose their own friends. Why can't I?

Mrs. Chopra: My dear, your father and I know what's best for you.

Sue: Mom, please...

Mrs. Chopra: You can't just go out with anybody. It's important to choose your friends carefully.

Sue: But Mom...

Mrs. Chopra: If your father and I don't know your friends, then you can see them at school only.

Sue: Well, it's not fair.

Mrs. Chopra: Maybe not. But that's how it is.

◆ EPISODE THREE

PART ONE

Sue: Hi, Neil.

Neil: Oh, hi, Sue. There you are. I didn't see you.

Sue: We've got half an hour before the movie starts. Why don't we walk through the park?

Neil: Sure.

Sue: So how are you doing?

Neil: Fine. How about you?

Sue: Fine. By the way, I hope my mother wasn't too rude to you on the phone.

Neil: No, of course not.

Sue: It's just that she was upset.

Neil: Well, of course she was upset. She didn't know who I was.

Sue: Well, I'm sorry.

Neil: That's all right. Don't worry about it.

Sue: Yeah, OK. But she always has to know who I'm with, where I'm going, when I'll be home...

Neil: Well, of course.

Sue: Mm. It's a shame Bob couldn't be here, isn't it?

Neil: Yeah, it is.

Sue: He's really fun, isn't he?

Neil: Yes, he is. Have you known him long?

Sue: Yeah, ages. We went to school together.

Neil: Really?

Sue: Yeah. And his dad knows my dad. He's been a friend of the family for years.

Neil: Oh, he's a family friend then?

Sue: Well... yes.

Neil: Do you often go to hockey games together?

Sue: Sure. About once a month.

Neil: Really. Just you two or...?

Sue: Sure. Or sometimes we go with other friends. What about you, Neil? Do you go out much?

Neil: Rarely. I'm too busy studying.

Sue: Neil! You should go out, have some fun!

Neil: That's what I'm doing now, isn't it?

Sue: Oh no! Look at this line.

Neil: Must be a good movie.

PART TWO

Neil: Hi, Dan. How are you doing?

Dan: I'm OK. What about you?

Neil: OK, I guess. I don't know.

Dan: Hey! What's the matter? Was the class that bad?

Neil: No, no. It was fine. It's something else. Dan, can I ask you something?

Dan: Sure. What is it?

Neil: Well, I've met this girl and...

Dan: Hey, who is she? What does she look like?

Neil: She's beautiful. She's called Sue. Her real name's Sushila.

Dan: So where did you meet her?

Neil: I met her at a hockey game last week.

Dan: Really?

Neil: Yes. That's the problem. She was with a guy from my math class. Bob.

Dan: Well, what's the problem? Maybe they're just friends.

Neil: Just friends? A man and a woman?

Dan: Yeah.

Neil: But they go out together a lot. She told me.

Dan: Well, why not? Men and women often go out together here.

Neil: Really?

Dan: Yeah. It doesn't mean they're dating or anything.

Neil: That's strange. In India that wouldn't happen. So what should I do?

Dan: Well, why don't you ask her out on a date?

Neil: But I'm not sure if Bob is her boyfriend.

Dan: Well, if I were you, I'd ask her.

Neil: Well, I could but.... Oh no.

Dan: What? What's the matter?

Neil: There she is! There's Sue. And here comes Bob.

Dan: Where? Oh, I see.

Neil: Look! See what I mean? They're hugging.

Dan: But Neil...

PART THREE

Neil: Hello?

Sue: Neil. Hi.

Neil: Hello.

Sue: It's me...Sue.

Neil: Hi, Sue.

Sue: Are you OK?

Neil: Sure. Why?

Sue: Oh, I don't know. You sound strange.

Neil: No, I'm fine.

Sue: Good. I was wondering...would you like to do something Saturday?

Neil: Saturday. Well, what were you thinking of?

Sue: Well, there's a new exhibit at the art gallery. Emily Carr.

Neil: Oh?

Sue: Yeah. I just love her paintings. Would you like to go?

Neil: Well...I don't know. I'm really busy. I've got a paper I have to finish by Sunday night.

Sue: Neil the bookworm! Take a break. It will do you good.

Neil: Is Bob going, too?

Sue: Bob? Well no, I haven't asked him. Why?

Neil: I just wondered. Well...OK then. What time?

Sue: How about getting there before the crowds, say about ten?

Neil: Ten. Yeah, that's fine. Where should we meet?

Sue: Let's meet somewhere near the gallery.

Neil: OK. Why don't we meet inside then?

Sue: All right.

Neil: OK. Saturday then.

Sue: OK. Are you sure you're OK?

Neil: Yes, of course. Bye.

Sue: Oh. Bye.

◆ EPISODE FOUR

PART ONE

Sue: Neil!

Neil: Hi.

Sue: How are you?

Neil: Fine.

Sue: Did you have any trouble finding the gallery?

Neil: No. No trouble.

Sue: Oh, that's good. Neil, is something wrong?

Neil: Wrong? No. Why?

Sue: Well, you seem... different.

Neil: Different?

Sue: Yeah, and you sounded strange on the phone, too. What's going on?

Neil: Well, actually, I, I...

Sue: Yes. Tell me. Did something happen?

Neil: Yes... well, no. I mean, it's just that...

Sue: You can tell me.

Neil: Well, I saw you and Bob at school.

Sue: Did you? I didn't see you.

Neil: Yes, and you were... you were hugging.

Sue: Yes, and what happened?

Neil: Well, that's it. You were hugging.

Sue: I don't get it. What's wrong with hugging?

Neil: Well, I just felt that, well, maybe you and Bob, you know...

Sue: Oh, Neil! I get it! No! We're just friends. Don't worry about Bob and me.

Neil: But why were you hugging?

Sue: Well, Bob got some really good news. His sister had a baby! And I was happy for him, so I...

Neil: Oh, I see.

Sue: There's nothing between us.

Neil: There isn't?

Sue: No. I'm *not* Bob's girlfriend.

Neil: You aren't?

Sue: No! And I'm sorry about the misunderstanding.

Neil: No, no. *I'm* sorry, Sue. I didn't understand. Things are so different here.

Sue: I know, but don't worry. Come on! Let's see the exhibit.

PART TWO

Sue: Let's look at Exhibit A first.

Neil: Sure. OK.

Sue: How do you like this one? It's called *Wood Interior*.

Neil: Hmm. It's interesting. I like it. How much is it?

Sue: Let's see. It's $80,000.

Neil: $80,000! Gee, that's a lot of money.

Sue: Well, Emily Carr's very popular.

Neil: $80,000 would pay for, let me see, well, lots of trips to India, anyway.

Sue: Let's go see Carr's early work. I think it's on the second floor, but I'm not sure.

Neil: OK.

Sue: Just let me ask this guy for directions.

Neil: OK.

Sue: Excuse me. Can you tell me where Emily Carr's early work is?

Attendant: Sure. It's on the second floor. Take the elevator next to the men's restroom...

Sue: Next to the men's restroom?

Attendant: That's right. When you get off the elevator, turn right. Walk past Exhibit D.

Sue: Exhibit D?

Attendant: Yes. And then go left...

Sue: Left.

Attendant: Yes. Walk to the end of the hall and turn left again. It's in Exhibit E.

Sue: Thanks.

Attendant: You're welcome.

Sue: So, Neil, when are you going back to India?

Neil: When my visa expires, in a few months.

Sue: Really! So soon!

Neil: I don't want to go, but...

Sue: You don't? Why not?

Neil: Why not? Well, I met you. I want to stay, but I don't know how it'll be possible.

Sue: Well, why don't you extend your student visa? Can't you do that?

Neil: It's possible. But I have to show I have enough money to continue studying here.

Sue: Is that a problem?

Neil: Well, I don't think my parents have enough money to pay for any more courses.

Sue: Oh, I see. That's too bad. Well, can you work? Maybe get a job at the university?

Neil: It's hard. Lots of people apply for work. I'm going to try, but the chances aren't good.

Sue: Well, there must be another way. I know, Neil! You could always have a marriage of convenience.

Neil: Do you really think so?

Sue: Neil! I was only kidding! I think marriages of convenience are wrong!

PART THREE

Sue: I enjoyed the exhibit. How about you?

Neil: It was very interesting. Thanks for inviting me.

Sue: Oh, you're welcome. Thanks for coming.

Neil: Do you have to go home now?

Sue: No. Why?

Neil: Well, why don't we go out for...

Sue: Coffee? Sure. There's a nice place a few blocks from here.

Neil: Great!

Sue: Oh, no!

Neil: What?!

Sue: It's my mother. Oh, no! She saw us! Here she comes.

Neil: Uh-oh. What should I do?

Sue: Nothing, nothing. It's too late.

Mrs. Chopra: Sushila!

Sue: Mom! What a surprise! This is my friend Neil, Mom. Neil, this is my mother, Pia Chopra.

Neil: How do you do, Mrs. Chopra.

Mrs. Chopra: How do you do. Sushila, what are you doing?

Sue: Well, Neil and I went to an art exhibit. We were just going to have coffee.

Neil: Yes, yes, that's right. Would you like to join us?

Mrs. Chopra: No, thank you. Sushila, I think you'd better come home with me.

Sue: But Mom, we're going to have coffee. Why don't you come with us?

Mrs. Chopra: Sushila, I will not argue here on the street.

Sue: But, Mom! I can't just leave Neil here.

Mrs. Chopra: Neil, do you know your way home?

Neil: Oh, yes, yes. No problem.

Mrs. Chopra: All right then. Good-bye, Neil.

Sue: Mom!

Mrs. Chopra: Come along, Sushila!

Sue: Neil, I'm so sorry.

Neil: It's all right. Bye.

Sue: Bye.

◆ EPISODE FIVE

PART ONE

Neil: So, what happened with your mom?

Sue: Well, I had a big argument with her, and now I'm grounded!

Neil: Grounded? What do you mean?

Sue: Well, I can't go out...except to school. I shouldn't even be here right now!

Waitress: Excuse me. Would you like anything else here?

Sue: Not for me, thanks.

Neil: Uh, no thanks.

Sue: And...and, my parents are starting to look for a husband for me!

Neil: Really?! An arranged marriage?

Sue: That's right.

Neil: Is that what you want?

Sue: No! I want to find my own husband, and...

Neil: And?

Sue: And I want to keep seeing you. I'm comfortable with you.

Neil: I feel the same way about you. But if you're grounded...

Waitress: Excuse me. Here's your bill. Thank you very much.

Neil: Thank you.

Sue: I can handle that. I've been grounded before. *I'm* worried about the arranged marriage.

Neil: Me too! But, listen. I have bad news, too.

Sue: What?

Neil: Well, I talked to someone about a job here.

Sue: Yeah, and...

Neil: Well, he said there's no chance.

Sue: Oh, no! That's too bad.

Neil: Yeah, there are about 200 people for ten jobs!

Sue: Wow! That's incredible. So, now what?

Neil: I don't know. Listen. How much of a tip should I leave?

Sue: Depends on how the service was—around 15 percent usually.

Neil: So, a dollar? Is that enough?

Sue: Hmm. Let me see the bill. Two coffees, a dollar fifty; two cakes, five dollars. That's six fifty. So, yeah, a dollar is fine.

Neil: OK. Well, do you want to go?

Sue: Yeah, we'd better. My mom's probably waiting for me.

PART TWO

Bob: Sue! Sue!

Sue: Bob! Hi. How are you?

Bob: Much better. How are you doing?

Sue: Oh, you know. Same old story. My mom grounded me.

Bob: Grounded!? At your age? You can't be serious!

Sue: Oh, I'm serious, all right.

Bob: Well, that's too bad, 'cause I'm having a party Saturday night. And you're invited.

Sue: Really!? Sounds good. What kind of party?

Bob: Well, I've asked everybody to bring something to eat or drink, so...

Sue: A potluck! Great!

Bob: Yeah. I've invited about twenty people, including Neil!

Sue: Oh, no. I'd really like to come, but I'm not supposed to see any guys except at school. What should I do?

Bob: I don't know, Sue. You have to do what you think is right.

Sue: You know, I really like Neil. I'm not interested in anyone else.

Bob: And how does Neil feel?

Sue: He says he feels the same way.

Bob: Is that right? That's great. So when's the wedding?

Sue: It's not funny! My parents are already looking for a husband for me!

Bob: Oh, so you're really stuck.

Sue: I am. I love my parents, but...

Bob: But you want to be with Neil.

Sue: That's right. And I feel guilty lying to my mom.

Bob: Well, that's too bad, Sue. I hope you can work it out.

Sue: I will. But anyway, I have to go. I'll come to the party, somehow.

Bob: Great. I'll see you Saturday.

Sue: Wait! What should I bring?

Bob: Hey. It's a potluck, a *real* one. Bring whatever you want!

PART THREE

Liz: How do you know this, Dan?

Dan: He told me, Liz.

Liz: Really! He told you?!

Dan: Yeah. Well, he's in one of my classes...

Liz: Yeah?

Dan: And he told me he really wants to stay here.

Liz: Where's he from?

Dan: I'm not sure. And he's going to ask her to marry him.

Liz: Does he love her?

Dan: Are you kidding, Liz?! Of course not. He just wants to immigrate.

Student: Sshhh!

Liz: Oh, that's terrible. Does she know?

Dan: No way!

Liz: Well, who is she?

Dan: I don't know her, but she's a student here.

Liz: Poor thing. Somebody should tell her.

Dan: You're right. But who?

Student: Ssshhhhh!

Liz: You should talk to him, Dan.

Dan: And say what?

Liz: Tell him...I don't know, that he should tell her the truth.

Dan: Liz, you're crazy! Then she'd never marry him.

Liz: Yeah, I guess so.

Dan: Anyway, he won't listen to me.

Student: This is a library! Sssssshhhhh!!!!!

◆ EPISODE SIX

PART ONE

Bob: Hey, Sue! You're late.

Sue: I almost didn't make it. But I'm here now.

Bob: Great. Can I get you a drink?

Sue: Sure.

Bob: What would you like? Beer, red wine, white wine, juice?

Sue: White wine, please.

Bob: OK.

Neil: Sue! I've missed you.

Sue: Mm. Me, too. I wasn't sure I'd be here, but...

Bob: Hey, you two! Cut it out. Where do you think you are?

Neil: Oh. Sorry, Bob.

Bob: No, no. I was joking. Here's your wine, Sue.

Sue: Thanks. Oh...whoops! I've spilled some on your carpet.

Bob: Don't worry about it. Neil, your glass is empty. Can I get you a beer?

Neil: Oh, no thanks. I don't drink.

Bob: Well, some juice then?

Neil: Juice would be fine. Thanks.

Bob: Sure.

Neil: Hey, there's Dan. Come on, Sue. I want you to meet him.

Sue: OK. He looks familiar.

Neil: Dan!

Dan: Hi, Neil. Having fun?

Neil: Now I am. Dan, this is Sue.

Dan: Hi, Sue. I've heard a lot about you.

Sue: Hi. Really?

Dan: Oh, yes. Neil's in love! I don't think he'll ever want to go back to India.

Sue: Well, I hope not.

Neil: Dan!

Dan: He's doing his best to stay here.

Sue: I know.

Bob: Here you are, Neil.

Neil: Thanks, Bob.

Bob: Now...do you guys want some food? There's lots here.

Sue: Not right now, thanks.

Bob: What?! Lost your appetite, Sue? You know what that means!

Sue: Bob!

PART TWO

Sue: Hasn't this been great, being together?

Neil: Yes. And knowing that we won't run into your mother!

Sue: We'd better help Bob clean up. Need a hand, Bob?

Bob: No, no. You two just enjoy yourselves...while you can. Dan's helping.

Neil: When do you have to be home, Sue?

Sue: Soon. But not yet.

Neil: Oh, Sue. What are we going to do?

Sue: I don't know, Neil. Anyway, it looks like you'll be going back to India pretty soon, doesn't it?

Neil: Well, not necessarily. Something may turn up.

Sue: Mm. Maybe.

Neil: Or maybe there's another way.

Sue: Like what?

Neil: Uh, well, I don't know.

Sue: Neither do I.

Neil: Sue, you know I love you.

Sue: Oh, Neil. I know. And I love you, too. But what can we do?

Neil: Well, if we love each other...uh...we could uh...

Sue: What?

Neil: Well, what I'm trying to say is...you know...well, why don't we get married?

Sue: But, Neil...

Neil: Sue, I'm asking you...will you marry me?

PART THREE

Neil: Sue. Come in. You're early.

Sue: So, this is where you live!

Neil: Mm.

Sue: Neil. What's wrong? Are you sick?

Neil: Yes. I think I have the flu.

Sue: Too much partying, you mean!

Neil: I feel awful.

Sue: Do you have a fever?

Neil: I think so.

Sue: Do you have any aspirin?

Neil: No.

Sue: Your head feels really hot. You'd better see a doctor.

Neil: A doctor?

Sue: Yeah. Do you have one?

Neil: No. I've never been to a doctor here before.

Sue: Well, I know a good one. Let me call and make you an appointment.

Neil: Well...OK.

Receptionist: Good afternoon. Dr. Cooper's office.

Sue: Yes. I'd like to make an appointment with Dr. Cooper. It's for a friend of mine.

Receptionist: OK. And what's the problem?

Sue: I think he has the flu.

Receptionist: How would tomorrow—Thursday—at nine in the morning be?

Sue: Tomorrow at nine. Uh...yes, that's fine.

Receptionist: And what's the name?

Sue: Neil Chandra. C-h-a-n-d-r-a.

Receptionist: Chandra. Tomorrow at nine then.

Sue: Thank you. Good-bye. So your appointment's at nine tomorrow. OK?

Neil: OK. Thanks, Sue. Sue, have you thought about my proposal?

Sue: Yes. But first of all, let me go to the drugstore and get you some aspirin for that fever. OK?

Neil: But, Sue...what's your answer?

Sue: We'll talk about it when I get back, Neil.

◆ *EPISODE SEVEN*

PART ONE

Sue: Neil! I'm back! Can I make some tea for you?

Neil: Sure, that'd be great.

Sue: Oh, you're on the phone.

Neil: I'll just be a minute.

Sue: OK. I'll go make the tea.

Neil: Are there any other ways I can immigrate?

Neil: My wife can sponsor me. I see. How does that work?

Neil: She has to be a citizen or a permanent resident. OK.

Neil: She completes the application. Yes. Is that it?

Neil: Then we have an interview with an immigration counselor. OK. Well, thanks a lot.

Neil: Bye.

Sue: Here's the tea and some water for the aspirin.

Neil: That's great. Thanks, Sue.

Sue: You're welcome. Who were you talking to?

Neil: Oh, nobody. Let's not talk about it. I want to talk about your decision.

Sue: Decision? What decision?

Neil: You know what decision. Will you marry me?

Sue: Oh, that! Well, actually, I need more time to think about it.

Neil: More time? Why? What's wrong?

Sue: Nothing's wrong. I just need a little time. It's a big decision. That's all. OK?

Neil: Of course, of course. I just hope you decide soon.

PART TWO

Neil: I don't understand it, Dan! She wants more time to think about it!

Dan: Well, that's all right. At least she didn't say no.

Neil: Why does she need time? We're a perfect match.

Dan: That must be the pizza! I hope you're hungry.

Neil: I'm starving!

Dan: Hi. That's great. Thanks a lot. Here's yours, Neil—green pepper and mushroom.

Neil: Thanks. It's great to have take-out food. Nothing to clean up in the kitchen!

Dan: That's for sure. And I still can't cook very well!

Neil: Me neither. Hey, that looks good! What did you order?

Dan: Pepperoni and tomato. Have a piece.

Neil: Thanks. Anyway, look at our ages. Sue's twenty-one and I'm twenty-four.

Dan: But age isn't the most important thing, Neil.

Neil: Well, another thing, her parents are from India, so we have a lot in common!

Dan: That's true. But she's pretty westernized, too. Isn't that a problem?

Neil: No, that's no problem. *And*, she comes from a good family.

Dan: How do you know that?

Neil: Well, her mother really looks after her!

Dan: Neil, you haven't touched your pizza! Come on.

Neil: OK. OK.

Dan: But still Neil, what about the most important thing?

Neil: What? My parents? They'll love her. In fact, they're coming from India soon and . . . . Hey! This pizza is good.

Dan: Yeah, not bad. The best thing is it's two pizzas for the price of one! Anyway, parents *aren't* the most important thing.

Neil: Well, what then?

Dan: Well, Neil, do you *love* her?

PART THREE

Sue: He asked me to marry him.

Bob: Sue! That's wonderful! That's great! So?

Sue: So, I said I wanted to think about it.

Bob: Think about it!? I thought you loved him.

Sue: I do, I do. But something's really *bugging* me.

Bob: What's that?

Sue: Well, I'm not sure that he wants to marry me for the right reason.

Bob: Well, he loves you, doesn't he?

Sue: He *says* he does, but . . .

Bob: You know what's really bugging *me*?

Sue: What?

Bob: The smoke in this place. It's unbelievable.

Sue: I know. I wish they had room in the no-smoking section.

Bob: Me, too!

Sue: Anyway, I think he might just want to immigrate.

Bob: What? I can't believe it! Why do you say that?

Sue: Well, at the art gallery, he asked me how he could stay in the country.

Bob: Well, sure, because he doesn't know the system here.

Sue: But then he said that we could have a marriage of convenience.

Bob: But he was joking, right?

Sue: I thought so. But then I heard some people in the library talking.

Bob: Yeah?

Sue: And they were talking about this guy who's using this girl to immigrate.

Bob: And he doesn't really love her?

Sue: Right. Then I heard Neil talking to Immigration. But he didn't want to tell me who he was talking to.

Bob: Oh, no. And now he wants to marry you? This doesn't look good.

Sue: I know. What am I going to do?

Bob: You have to talk to Neil about it. Right away.

◆ EPISODE EIGHT

PART ONE

Loudspeaker: Trans-Ocean Airlines announces the arrival of flight number 264 from London. This is the last call for Maple Leaf Air passengers boarding flight number 447 to Vancouver. Maple Leaf Air passengers to Vancouver, please board through gate three.

Neil: Mother! Father! Over here!

Mrs. Chandra: Oh, Neil! My darling.

Neil: Mother! It's great to see you!

Mr. Chandra: Come here, my son!

Neil: Father! I'm so glad you're here.

Mr. Chandra: So are we.

Neil: How was your flight?

Mr. Chandra: Very long! And I wasn't able to sleep at all.

Mrs. Chandra: Neil! You've lost weight. You look too thin.

Neil: Well . . . I'm not the best cook in the world.

Mrs. Chandra: You need someone to look after you. So . . . have you thought about the young lady I wrote you about?

Neil: Well . . . I didn't think you were *that* serious.

Mr. Chandra: Oh, your mother's very serious, Neil!

Neil: Really?

Mr. Chandra: Yes. She really wants you to get married. I think she's ready for grandchildren.

Mrs. Chandra: Oh, you know, dear. I just want to see my son happy.

Mr. Chandra: Of course. I do, too.

Mrs. Chandra: So . . . will you meet this young lady?

Neil: You know I can't say no to you, Mother. But can we talk about it later? Let's go home.

Mr. Chandra: Good idea.

Neil: I borrowed a friend's car. It's right over there. Oh, no!

Mr. and Mrs. Chandra: What's the matter?!

Neil: I just got a parking ticket. I can see it on the windshield.

Mr. Chandra: That's too bad.

Mrs. Chandra: You go to the car, Neil. Your father and I will wait here with the suitcases.

Neil: OK. I'd better go before they tow the car away. I'll be right back.

PART TWO

Neil: Sue! What a surprise! What are you doing here?

Sue: I have a terrible headache. I came to buy some aspirin. What are *you* doing here?

Neil: Well, Dr. Cooper gave me a prescription for some antibiotics. She said I have strep throat.

Sue: That's why you had such a high fever.

Pharmacist: Can I help you?

Neil: Yes. I'd like to have this prescription filled.

Pharmacist: All right. Have you had other prescriptions filled here before?

Neil: No.

Pharmacist: What's your full name?

Neil: Neil Chandra. C-h-a-n-d-r-a.

Pharmacist: And your address, please?

Neil: It's 1-3-6-0 Cherrywood Road, number 17.

Pharmacist: And your phone number, please.

Neil: 683-2985.

Pharmacist: All right. It'll be about 15 minutes.

Neil: Thanks. Sue, I need to talk to you. It's *really* important.

Sue: Yes. What is it? Tell me!

Neil: Not here. Let's go to the park across the street.

Sue: OK. Let's sit over there.

Neil: Sure. Sue, my parents want me to marry an Indian girl that lives here.

Sue: You mean they're arranging a marriage for you!

Neil: Yes. Sue, I don't want to marry her. I want you! Please marry me!

Sue: You want to marry *me*!

Neil: Well, of course! I love you, Sue.

Sue: Oh, Neil . . . I feel so relieved.

Neil: Relieved? What do you mean?

Sue: Well . . . you see . . . I thought . . . maybe you wanted to marry me to stay in the country.

Neil: Sue! How could you think that?

Sue: Well . . . I heard you talking with an immigration officer the other day, and . . .

Neil: But Sue, don't you realize that I love you? I want to be with you *always*!

Sue: Oh, Neil . . .

Neil: I don't care where we live . . . here, India, anywhere, as long as we're together.

Sue: Neil, I feel like such a fool. How could I have suspected you?

Neil: So... Will you marry me?

Sue: Of course I'll marry you!

PART THREE

Mrs. Chopra: Sushila, be careful! Move that nail polish away from the burners.

Sue: OK, Mom.

Mrs. Chopra: You should never leave things like that close to the burners when you're cooking.

Sue: You're right. I'm sorry.

Mrs. Chopra: You know it could catch fire. It's flammable.

Sue: Mom, could I talk to you and Dad for a minute?

Mrs. Chopra: What is it, Sushila? Are you all right?

Sue: I'm fine. Can we go to the living room for a minute, please?

Mrs. Chopra: So, what's the problem, Sushila?

Sue: Mom, Dad, I've made a decision.

Mr. Chopra: Yes? What decision?

Sue: I'm in love with Neil, and I want to marry him.

Mrs. Chopra: Sushila! You can't do that!

Sue: Mom, please...

Mr. Chopra: You were told not to see him again!

Sue: I know, but...

Mrs. Chopra: You've continued to see that young man! You've disobeyed us!

Sue: Let me explain.

Mr. Chopra: There's nothing to explain! I'm very disappointed in you, Sushila.

Sue: But Dad...

Mr. Chopra: That's enough. There's nothing to talk about. We forbid you to see that young man *ever again*!

Sue: Dad, no!

Mrs. Chopra: Sushila, we've chosen a very nice young man for you. We'd like you to meet him. He comes from a very good family and...

Sue: I don't want to hear about it!

◆ *EPISODE NINE*

PART ONE

Bob: Oh, Sue, you're here. Finally!

Sue: I'm really sorry I'm late.

Bob: You're half an hour late. What happened? Are you OK?

Sue: Yes. I just missed my bus.

Bob: So tell me what's wrong.

Sue: I feel terrible!

Bob: Have you told your parents about your decision?

Sue: Yes, I have. And now I can't even see Neil anymore.

Bob: Really? Well, listen. I have an idea.

Sue: What?

Bob: I know it's crazy, but have you thought about eloping?

Sue: Eloping?! You mean...

Bob: Yes. Run away with Neil and marry him.

Sue: Are you serious?!

Bob: I know it's not the best thing to do... but if you love each other...

Sue: But what about my family? They'd never forgive me.

Bob: Well... what else can you do?

Sue: I don't know.

Bob: Why don't you talk about it with Neil?

Sue: I should, but I'm so scared. What if my parents see us together again?

Bob: How about calling him from here? Ask him to come to my apartment.

Sue: That's a great idea!

Bob: I'll go out and leave you two alone.

Sue: Thanks, Bob.

PART TWO

Sue: That must be Neil.

Bob: I'll get it.

Neil: Hello, Bob.

Bob: Hi. Come on in, Neil. I'm just on my way out. See you later.

Neil: See you.

Sue: Neil... I'm so glad to see you.

Neil: Sue. I feel terrible about your parents' reaction.

Sue: So do I. Neil, what are we going to do now?

Neil: Well... what if I tell my parents that I'm in love with you?

Sue: And then what?

Neil: Then I can ask them to talk to your parents.

Sue: It's useless. My parents would never listen.

Neil: Why not?

Sue: They've already made their decision.

Neil: So... what can we do?

Sue: Well... Bob suggested eloping, but...

Neil: No way! That's impossible. Our culture wouldn't allow that.

Sue: I know, but I love you, and I want to marry you.

Neil: And I want to marry *you*.

Sue: There must be something else we can do.

Neil: Yes, but what? Maybe *I* could talk to your parents. It might help.

Sue: Absolutely not! They'd never listen to you. It'll make things worse.

Neil: Well then, can *you* try to talk to them again?

Sue: That's impossible! They already told me there's nothing to talk about.

Neil: Sue, love. Then it's best that we don't see each other again.

Sue: I guess so.

Neil: I want you to know that I'll always love you.

Sue: And I'll always love *you*. I'll never forget you, Neil.

Neil: Good-bye, Sue.

Sue: Good-bye.

PART THREE

Mrs. Chopra: Before we go home, remind me to drop off the recyclable garbage.

Sue: OK.

Mrs. Chopra: Say, how about stopping at the East Indian Boutique first?

Sue: What for?

Mrs. Chopra: I want to buy you a new sari for the party.

Sue: What party?

Mrs. Chopra: Your father and I have organized a party for next Saturday.

Sue: Why?

Mrs. Chopra: For you to meet this young man we told you about and his parents.

Sue: Oh, OK.

Mrs. Chopra: Here we are.

Clerk: Good morning. May I help you?

Mrs. Chopra: Yes. We're looking for a sari for my daughter.

Clerk: What color?

Mrs. Chopra: Blue's our favorite.

Clerk: I just got in some very beautiful ones. Oh, here's a blue one.

Mrs. Chopra: It's lovely! Why don't you try it on?

Clerk: I'll get you a blouse. What size do you wear?

Sue: Seven.

Clerk: Here.

Mrs. Chopra: Oh! It's beautiful. What do you think, Sushila?

Sue: Yes. It's very nice.

Clerk: That color really suits you. How's the blouse?

Sue: It's a little tight.

Clerk: I'll get you a larger size. Here you are. How does that one feel?

Sue: It's better.

Mrs. Chopra: How much are they?

Clerk: They're on sale. The two pieces are $249 plus 10 percent tax.

Mrs. Chopra: That's fine. We'll take them.

Clerk: Will that be cash or charge?

Mrs. Chopra: Charge. Do you take VISTA?

Clerk: Yes. Of course. Sign here, please. Thank you and have a nice day.

Mrs. Chopra & Sue: You, too.

◆ *EPISODE TEN*

PART ONE

Mrs. Chopra: OK. The samosas and pakoras are ready.

Sue: Are we having all Indian food?

Mrs. Chopra: Yes, of course, dear. I've made some curries. I've made one lamb and one vegetable. You like lamb curry, don't you?

Sue: Yes.

Mrs. Chopra: And I made your favorite. These little coconut cookies. Here, try one.

Sue: No, thanks. I'm not hungry right now.

Mrs. Chopra: Are you feeling all right, Sushila?

Sue: Yes. I'm not hungry, that's all.

Mrs. Chopra: Now dear, I don't want you to be nervous about meeting these people.

Sue: I'm not nervous, Mom. I'm fine.

Mrs. Chopra: Well, that's good. They really are very nice people...Get that, will you, dear?

Sue: Hello.

Neil: Sue? This is Neil.

Sue: What are you doing? You can't call me here.

Neil: But Sue, listen. I have something to tell you. It's important.

Sue: I can't talk now. Bye.

Mrs. Chopra: Who was that?

Sue: Just a friend.

Mrs. Chopra: Oh. Well, you should change now. Our guests will be here soon.

Sue: Yes, Mother. I'm just going upstairs.

Mrs. Chopra: OK. I'll be up in a minute.

PART TWO

Mr. Chopra: Amit! It's wonderful to see you. Come in, come in.

Amit: I'm glad to see you, too, Dilip.

Mr. Chopra: And Monisha, my dear, how are you?

Monisha: Very well, thank you, Dilip. Where's Pia?

Mr. Chopra: She's upstairs with Sushila. They'll be down in a minute.

Monisha: I'm looking forward to meeting Sushila.

Amit: So, how long has it been since we saw you last, Dilip?

Mr. Chopra: Well, I left India nearly twenty-five years ago now, and I haven't seen you since then.

Amit: Twenty-five years!

Mr. Chopra: Yes. It's a long time. So where's your son?

Amit: He'll just be a minute. He's parking the car.

Mr. Chopra: He's still a student, isn't he?

Amit: Yes, but he'll be finished soon.

Mr. Chopra: And what then?

Amit: He's a smart young man. He'll get a good job.

Mr. Chopra: Good, good.

Amit: And what about Sushila? She's still studying, too, isn't she?

Mr. Chopra: Yes. She has another year to go. She's very busy with her studies.

Monisha: Like our oldest daughter, Tara. She works so hard.

Mr. Chopra: Yes, so how's your family?

Amit: Well, our other son and our two daughters are all in India. They're doing well.

Mr. Chopra: And are your parents still living with you?

Amit: Yes. And so are my brother Anil and his wife and their three children.

Mr. Chopra: Here come Pia and Sushila... And that must be your son.

PART THREE

Mrs. Chopra: Sushila, darling, could you get the door, please? My hands are full.

Sue: Neil!!! What are you doing here!?

Neil: Sue, let me explain.

Sue: Please go away! It's over between us.

Neil: Sue. I need to tell you something.

Mrs. Chandra: Neil, is that you, son?

Sue: Neil?! Your son?!

Mrs. Chandra: Of course. Come in. I want to introduce you to Mr. and Mrs. Chopra.

Mrs. Chopra: What seems to be the prob—

Mrs. Chandra: Pia, I'd like you to meet my son, Neil.

Mrs. Chopra: *Your son*?!

Sue: Yes, Mom. This is Neil!

Mrs. Chopra: I can't believe it!

Mrs. Chandra: You know each other?

Mrs. Chopra: Let me explain, Monisha. Sushila and Neil met at the university about six months ago.

Mrs. Chandra: Really?

Sue: Yes. We fell in love and wanted to get married.

Neil: That's right, but we decided not to see each other again because Sue's parents wanted her to marry someone else.

Mrs. Chandra: Now I understand.

Neil: Sue, when I realized that the girl my parents wanted me to marry was *you*, I tried to call you.

Sue: Oh. *That's* why you called me.

Neil: But you hung up on me.

Sue: I'm sorry, Neil. This is incredible! It's a dream come true!

Neil: Now we will *always* be together!

Mrs. Chopra: This is wonderful! It was your destiny to be together.

Mrs. Chandra: Yes. It was meant to be, not just a coincidence.

Sue: Yes! This is the happiest day of my life!

Neil: Let's celebrate!

Everyone: Yes! Let's celebrate.

Answer Key

◆ EPISODE ONE

PART ONE

HAVE YOU GOT IT?

a, b

CHECK IT OUT

2. Yes
3. No, Sushila is going to the hockey game with Bob.
4. Yes

DOUBLE-CHECK IT

c

BETWEEN THE LINES

1. b   2. a   3. b

PART TWO

HAVE YOU GOT IT?

B

CHECK IT OUT

2. Neil   3. Bob   4. Neil   5. Sue

DOUBLE-CHECK IT

2. 14   3. 6 and 7   4. 0   5. 18

WORK IT OUT

2. a   3. b   4. a

PART THREE

HAVE YOU GOT IT?

2. game   3. restaurant   4. movie

CHECK IT OUT

2. Yes   3. No, Neil has a student visa.   4. Yes
5. No, Neil will return to India in six months.

DOUBLE-CHECK IT

2. Bob   3. Sue   4. Neil

BODY LANGUAGE

1. b

WORK IT OUT

game, score, team, win

IN OTHER WORDS

2. a   3. b   4. a   5. b

◆ EPISODE TWO

PART ONE

THINK BACK

✔ = 3,5,6;   X = 2,4,7

HAVE YOU GOT IT?

2. Neil   3. Neil   4. Sue

CHECK IT OUT

2. No   3. No   4. Yes

DOUBLE-CHECK IT

a, c, f

WORK IT OUT

1. a   2. b

PART TWO

HAVE YOU GOT IT?

b

CHECK IT OUT

2. Bob   3. sick   4. 8   5. 2   6. 5

BETWEEN THE LINES

1. b   2. a   3. b

WORK IT OUT

a. 3   b. 6   c. 1
d. 4   e. 5   f. 2

PART THREE

HAVE YOU GOT IT?

Mrs. Chopra and Sushila are arguing. Mrs. Chopra is angry about NEIL and Sushila going to the MOVIE. Sushila is UNHAPPY because she is NOT allowed to do what she wants.

CHECK IT OUT

2. Yes   3. Yes
4. No. Sushila can't choose her boyfriends.   5. Yes

DOUBLE-CHECK IT

a. 2   b. 1   c. 3

BETWEEN THE LINES

1. c   2. b

IN OTHER WORDS

1. a. become friends with   **b.** unreasonable
c. you don't have another choice

BODY LANGUAGE

1. a, b, d

◆ *EPISODE THREE*

PART ONE

THINK BACK

2. T   **3.** F. Neil speaks to Sue's mother on the phone.
4. F. Neil says Bob can't go to the movie.   **5.** T

HAVE YOU GOT IT?

I went out with NEIL. It was great. We walked through the park and then went to a MOVIE. We talked about all kinds of things. I apologized for my MOM. Neil understood why she was UNHAPPY about his call. He asked a lot of questions about BOB. I don't know why.

CHECK IT OUT

2. a   **3.** a   **4.** b   **5.** a

DOUBLE-CHECK IT

2. Always   **3.** Often   **4.** Sometimes   **5.** Rarely

BETWEEN THE LINES

1. No   **2.** Yes

PART TWO

HAVE YOU GOT IT?

c

CHECK IT OUT

a, c, d, e

BETWEEN THE LINES

1. c   **2.** b

WORK IT OUT

1. a, c, e

PART THREE

HAVE YOU GOT IT?

b

CHECK IT OUT

B

DID YOU GET THAT?

1. a   **2.** c   **3.** e

BETWEEN THE LINES

1. b   **2.** b

◆ *EPISODE FOUR*

PART ONE

THINK BACK

1. a   **2.** a   **3.** b

HAVE YOU GOT IT?

c

CHECK IT OUT

1. T   **2.** F. Sue tells Neil she is not Bob's girlfriend.
3. T

DOUBLE-CHECK IT

1. c   **2.** b

IN OTHER WORDS

1. a   **2.** b   **3.** a

PART TWO

TAKE A GUESS

1. art   **2.** Neil

HAVE YOU GOT IT?

b, c

CHECK IT OUT

1. a   **2.** b   **3.** a

DOUBLE-CHECK IT

Art Gallery Floor Plan

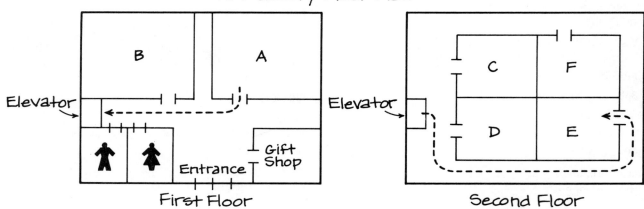

First Floor

Second Floor

IN OTHER WORDS

1. a   **2.** b   **3.** a

BETWEEN THE LINES

1. a   **2.** a

PART THREE

TAKE A GUESS

1. a   **2.** a   **3.** b

CHECK IT OUT

1. Yes   **2.** Yes   **3.** Yes   **4.** No. Neil goes home alone.

DOUBLE-CHECK IT

1. Sushila, Neil, Mrs. Chopra   **2.** Sushila
3. Sushila, Neil   **4.** Mrs. Chopra   **5.** Sushila

BETWEEN THE LINES

1. b   **2.** a

◆ EPISODE FIVE

PART ONE

THINK BACK

Mom saw <u>NEIL</u> and me outside the gallery. She was really <u>ANGRY</u>. Too bad! Neil and I had such a <u>GOOD</u> time there. I really <u>LIKE</u> him. I think he likes me, too. He was jealous of <u>BOB</u>.

HAVE YOU GOT IT?

a, c, d, f

CHECK IT OUT

a. 4   **b.** 1   **c.** 5   **d.** 2   **e.** 3

DOUBLE-CHECK IT

2. c   **3.** a   **4.** f   **5.** b   **6.** d

IN OTHER WORDS

1. b   **2.** b   **3.** b

PART TWO

TAKE A GUESS

1. Bob   **2.** Neil   **3.** parents

HAVE YOU GOT IT?

1. grounded   **2.** party

CHECK IT OUT

1. No. Bob doesn't think Sue should be grounded.
2. Yes
3. Yes
4. Yes
5. No. Sue doesn't want to date other men.

DOUBLE-CHECK IT

1. upset   **2.** sorry   **3.** guilty

IN OTHER WORDS

1. a   **2.** b   **3.** a   **4.** a

WORK IT OUT

Sue,

Don't forget I'm having a potluck party at my place on Saturday. Bring anything you want. See you there.
Bob

WHAT'S THE WORD?

1. Sue   **2.** husband   **4.** wedding   **5.** Bob
6. potluck   **7.** grounded

BETWEEN THE LINES

1. a   **2.** b

PART THREE

HAVE YOU GOT IT?

b

CHECK IT OUT

1. Yes   **2.** Yes   **3.** No   **4.** Yes

DOUBLE-CHECK IT

b, c

BODY LANGUAGE

1. b

◆ EPISODE SIX

PART ONE

THINK BACK

2. Neil   **3.** Bob   **4.** Dan

HAVE YOU GOT IT?

a, c, d

CHECK IT OUT

Bob: Some <u>juice</u>?

Neil: <u>Juice</u> would be fine. Thanks.

Dan: I've <u>heard</u> alot about you.

Sue: Really?

Dan: Yes. Neil's in <u>love</u>.

DID YOU GET THAT?

1. b   **2.** a   **3.** b

IN OTHER WORDS

2. a   **3.** f   **4.** g   **5.** h

BETWEEN THE LINES

1. b   **2.** b

WORK IT OUT

I. 1. a   **2.** b
II. 1. Ouch!   **2.** Phew!   **3.** Yuck!

PART TWO

HAVE YOU GOT IT?

a

CHECK IT OUT

1. No **2.** No **3.** Yes **4.** Yes **5.** Yes

IN OTHER WORDS

2. f **3.** a **4.** g

PART THREE

HAVE YOU GOT IT?

a, c

CHECK IT OUT

1. a **2.** a

DOUBLE-CHECK IT

THURSDAY 8	
9:00	Chandra
9:15	Basterfield
9:30	
9:45	Haiselden
10:00	Chung
10:15	
10:30	Morano
10:45	
11:00	
11:15	
11:30	
11:45	Valentin
1:00	Chadwick
1:15	

WORK IT OUT

1. a, b, e

◆ EPISODE SEVEN

PART ONE

THINK BACK

2. tell **3.** kill **4.** love **5.** arrange

HAVE YOU GOT IT?

1. b **2.** a

CHECK IT OUT

a, b, d, e

DOUBLE-CHECK IT

1. Yes

2. No. His wife can sponsor him if she's a citizen or a permanent resident.

3. Yes

4. Yes

PART TWO

HAVE YOU GOT IT?

a

CHECK IT OUT

a, b, d, e

IN OTHER WORDS

1. b **2.** b **3.** a **4.** a

BODY LANGUAGE

1. b

WORK IT OUT

b. 3 **c.** 5 **d.** 6 **e.** 2 **f.** 4

PART THREE

HAVE YOU GOT IT?

a

CHECK IT OUT

1, 3, 4, 5

BETWEEN THE LINES

1. a **2.** a **3.** b

IN OTHER WORDS

2. f **3.** b **4.** c **5.** a

◆ EPISODE EIGHT

PART ONE

THINK BACK

1. immigrating **2.** Dan **3.** Bob

CHECK IT OUT

3, 2, 1

DOUBLE-CHECK IT

1. 264, 447 **2.** 3

IN OTHER WORDS

1. b **2.** b **3.** a

PART TWO

HAVE YOU GOT IT?

1. Neil **2.** park **3.** parents **4.** marry **5.** yes

CHECK IT OUT

1. No. Sue went to the drugstore because she has a headache.

2. No. Sue has a bad headache./No. Neil has strep throat.

3. Yes
4. No. Neil hasn't had a prescription filled at that drugstore before.

DOUBLE-CHECK IT

1. b   **2.** c   **3.** b   **4.** b

BETWEEN THE LINES

1. a   **2.** b

PART THREE

TAKE A GUESS

2. talk   **3.** parents   **4.** important

HAVE YOU GOT IT?

a

CHECK IT OUT

1. safety   **2.** disagree   **3.** forbid   **4.** unhappy

DOUBLE-CHECK IT

1. b   **2.** b

◆ EPISODE NINE

PART ONE

THINK BACK

1. Neil   **2.** Mrs. Chandra   **3.** Sue   **4.** Sue
5. Mr. Chopra

HAVE YOU GOT IT?

b, c

CHECK IT OUT

1. b   **2.** a   **3.** a

DOUBLE-CHECK IT

1. F. Sue feels unhappy when she gets to Bob's apartment.
2. T
3. T
4. T
5. F. Bob won't stay with Sue and Neil while they talk.

PART TWO

HAVE YOU GOT IT?

Sue and Neil decide not to see each other again.

CHECK IT OUT

1. Yes
2. No. Neil leaves Bob's apartment.
3. No. Sue breaks out crying.

DOUBLE-CHECK IT

2. agrees   **3.** disagrees   **4.** disagrees   **5.** agrees

PART THREE

TAKE A GUESS

In Picture 2:
1. Mrs. Chopra is not wearing earrings.
2. Mrs. Chopra has an expression of dislike on her face.
3. Sue is not wearing any shoes.
4. The price tag on the sari reads $300.
5. The store clerk is not wearing glasses.
6. There is no hanger on the floor.

HAVE YOU GOT IT?

Picture 1

CHECK IT OUT

2. recyclable   **3.** Saturday   **4.** sari   **5.** husband

DOUBLE-CHECK IT

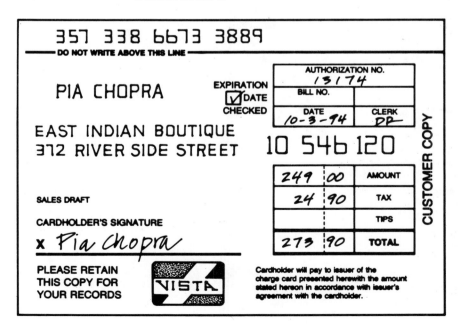

BODY LANGUAGE

1. a

◆ *EPISODE TEN*

PART ONE

THINK BACK

I met Bob today. He suggested that NEIL and I elope. What an idea! Anyway, NEIL came over to Bob's apartment, and we talked. Neil and I decided we should NOT stay together. I feel so SAD. Later MOM took me shopping for a new SARI. They're having a party for me to meet my future HUSBAND.

HAVE YOU GOT IT?

a. 3   **b.** 2   **c.** 1

CHECK IT OUT

1. F. The food Mrs. Chopra prepared is Indian.
2. T
3. F. Sushila does not try her mother's cookies.
4. T
5. T

DOUBLE-CHECK IT

1. c
2. b

BETWEEN THE LINES

1. happy
2. unhappy
3. upset
4. excited

WORK IT OUT

1. a. appetizers   **b.** main dish   **c.** dessert
2. Yes. Positive words: delicious, tasty, delectable, tasty

PART TWO

HAVE YOU GOT IT?

B

CHECK IT OUT

1. Mr. Chopra   **2.** Sushila   **3.** Amit's son
4. Amit's son   **5.** Sushila

DOUBLE-CHECK IT

2. 1   **3.** 2   **4.** 3   **5.** 3

WORK IT OUT

2. Anil   **3.** 3   **4.** Monisha   **5.** 3   **6.** Monisha
7. 2

PART THREE

HAVE YOU GOT IT?

1. Sushila   **2.** Neil   **3.** future husband

CHECK IT OUT

1. a   **2.** c

DOUBLE-CHECK IT

1. No. Mrs. Chopra asks Sue to answer the door.
2. No. Neil tries to tell Sue something.
3. Yes
4. Yes
5. Yes